Endorsements

"I have known Jim for over thirty years and witnessed the heart he has for others many times. Being in the NFL for ten years gave me opportunities to see what some of my teammates faced in the areas of prejudice and racism. I hope this book will stir up healthy conversations on the subject that will lead to meaningful change in hearts everywhere."

Rolf Benirschke—Former NFL kicker for San Diego Chargers, former daytime host of Wheel of Fortune, author of *Alive and Kicking* and popular motivational speaker.

"My parents were racists. The "n" word was commonplace in my home. When you're raised that way the seeds of latent racism get buried way down deep. I didn't put that stuff in there but I've had a heck of a time getting it out. Jim's Adkins' provocative book showed me there's a little more work to do."

Jay Carty—Played for Oregon State Basketball and several pro teams, including the L.A. Lakers. He coached with John Wooden at U.C.L.A, coaching Lew Alcindor (Kareem Abdul-Jabbar). He is the author of nine devotional books, including one based on John Wooden's pyramid of success.

"...Is RACISM a word that has burned indelibly negative connotations in your mind? Is it a subject you're reluctant to discuss beyond the borders of your own private universe? If so, prepare to step into a sociological mine field with Jim as he relates personally distasteful experiences which may help you recall some of yours in this first hand walk where so many fear to tread. Hopefully, his insights might provide you with the keys that'll unlock the manacles of your mind and allow you to assist others to do so as well. Perhaps then we'll witness the kind of progress necessary to put this country on the road to eventual equality."

Eddie Doucette—President of Doucette Promotions Inc. thirty years in NBA broadcasting, plus play by play radio and TV announcing for numerous pro sports including the San Diego Padres, the L.A. Clippers, the LA Rams.

"Jim experienced firsthand, as a San Jose State runner and student in the late '60s, the heart of America's young rebels' strong stance against racism. His reflections on that historic era of social change in our country and special time in track and field are compelling reading for track and field fans and for those studying sociology. *Speed City* remains a unique story in USA track and field annals."

Larry Knuth—California Community College Track & Field Hall of Fame inductee, and publisher/co-author/author of six track and field books (LK Publications).

"Playing major league baseball for thirteen years gave me the opportunity to observe firsthand the inequities the Black and Latin players faced throughout the season. They were treated with respect while in uniform and on the field, but in some situations with disdain while off the field. The issues in Jim's book are ones we need to continue to seek resolution for in our country. During my thirty years of friendship with Jim I came to realize two things. First, I knew from the beginning that Jim cared about me. And secondly, I have come to realize that Jim cares about everyone. I love the guy."

Tom Griffin—Former Major League pitcher. During his thirteen seasons, he played for the Astros, Padres, Angels, Giants and Pirates during his career. Tom and his wife Lorri own and operate Your Accessory Source.

Life Lessons From

speed
city

Insights From Track
and Field About Racism

By
Jim Adkins

*Jim
Keep up the good ministry
at Rose Drive. Thanks for
the friendship.
Jim
6-11*

IPG

Life Lessons From Speed City
Published by:
Intermedia Publishing Group, Inc.
P.O. Box 2825
Peoria, Arizona 85380
www.intermediapub.com

ISBN 978-1-935906-26-1

Table of Contents

Dedication

This book is dedicated to all the men and women who have served in the United States military, fighting for and defending the Constitution of the United States of America.

Also, this book is dedicated to my granddaughters, Jenna and Jillian Gomez. May they and their generation do a better job of understanding and living out the Pledge of Allegiance, truly seeing *Liberty and Justice for All*.

II   LIFE LESSONS FROM SPEED CITY

Acknowledgments

Special thanks to:

Marleen Adkins

Larry and June Knuth

Roxanne Young

Art and Angie Booth

Rolfe Benirschke

Eddie Doucette

Jay Carty

James S. Adkins

Tom Griffin

Lorenzo Romar

Rob White

Jeff Kroot

Dave Zirin

Ed Fox, *Track and Field News*

Liberty Board Shop

Toby Adkins

Ed Frank

Arnell Motz

Larry Lukas

Ken Kemp

Mylah Stanton

Robbie Adkins

Dave Funderburk

Art Wray

Bob Kraning

Ernestine Goldstein

Roy Halberg

Jim Conway

Photos:

Speed City on cover—Jeff Kroot

Jim Adkins on front cover—Dave Funderburk

Jim Adkins on back cover—Rob White

Foreword

With God using so many leaders to bring the message of racial reconciliation across our country and with so many individuals coming forward at conferences to become "reconciled" why are so few people experiencing a real covenant relationship with a brother or sister of a different cultural background? Why are so few churches becoming truly multi-ethnic? And why are so few cities being impacted to the degree that the press does not have a race riot or protest to report after a major crime is committed? What we must realize is that reconciliation messages and meetings while important are only the starting point. *Life Lessons from Speed City* is about a journey into a new self understanding of the impact of racism on our culture.

My heart has been to bring racial reconciliation to our nation. I recognize the scars are deep and not easily healed. When slavery ended, ownership ceased, but love and compassion did not fill in the gap. Instead, bitterness and resentment did, ushering in an era of division marked by hatred and abuse.

The fact that Africans were brought here against their will, indentured to a life of hard labor and treated less than human should make us all shudder. This country was built on the backs of these men and women. The economy soared in a way that would have been impossible without slavery. The United States got off to a great start as a world supplier of goods because of slave labor.

It is impossible to turn back the clock and change history. Mankind has a long history of men taking advantage of other men for their own gain that started way before the United States. It is unfortunate that our history is blighted with the poor treatment of fellow human beings. Industry in both the North and the South had become dependent on free labor, making the ending of slavery a major problem for everyone. Over 620 thousand Americans lost their lives fighting the battle over 3.5 million slaves.

The freeing of the slaves brought joy initially to the Negroes and their supporters, but then led to new kind of hardship. Southerners were so embittered at the forced loss of their income and work force, it seems they determined to make life miserable for the freed men and women. Being uneducated and poor, they had no place to live, no source of income and were either left to wander about or forced to join a one-sided share cropping plan. The feelings of hatred, resentment and distrust were being established. We still live with the residual problems of the poor handling of one of U.S. history's greatest human rights violations. The needed change was handled poorly.

In his inaugural speech, President Abraham Lincoln spoke about the need for love for one another in anticipation of the collision of ideals in the future. He said, "We are not enemies, but friends. We must not be enemies. Though passion may have strained it must not break our bonds of affection. The mystic chords of memory, stretching from every battlefield and patriot grave to every living heart and hearthstone all over this broad land, will yet swell the chorus of the Union, when again touched, as surely they will be, by the better angels of our nature." *Abraham Lincoln, March 4, 1861, From His First Inaugural Address.*

Our passion did strain our bonds of affection and they were broken. We are waiting to be touched by the better angels of nature.

Politicians have tried and made necessary laws to try and rectify the inequality of education, housing and employment. Some of the efforts have been successful, some have further entrenched each side. Politicians will continue to make laws in an effort to make things better, but most will fail, sadly. Politics is not the answer.

The challenge presented in *Life Lessons from Speed City* is not to look at "tolerance" as the goal, but to go beyond tolerance to love and compassion. I firmly believe that only through a spiritual awakening that opens men's hearts will we ever see meaningful change. Through transformation of hearts that leads to a new way of viewing ourselves and culture can we learn to really love one another.

Everyone can take something from this book. No matter what faith, or non-faith you might be, please take an inventory of your heart and identify any need for growth and change. Life is too short to live it with anything but love in our hearts and compassion for fellow men.

—Bishop Phillip H. Porter, Jr., former Chairman of Promise Keepers and founder of All Nations Pentecostal Church of God in Christ in Aurora, Colorado.

VIII   LIFE LESSONS FROM SPEED CITY

Prologue

Racism is alive and as robust in the twenty-first century as ever. This is a sad truth about our culture.

The city of San Jose was called "Speed City." Speed City had one of the greatest collection of sprinters ever assembled and they were all either running for or training at San Jose State. There were so many fast sprinters that sometimes a 9.4 100-yard dash time would not get you a lane in a dual meet. There was speed: both quality and quantity. There were Olympic gold medalists, Olympic record holders, world, American, and NCAA record-holders.

Speed City is remembered for more than Olympic Gold Medals, fast times and records during this era of world-class sprinters training together at San Jose. Depending on your point of view, Speed City is most famous, or infamous, for the social and racial advances made by these sprinters. These world-class runners used their success and fame to bring attention to one of America's ugliest issues: racism. Also, the focal point of much of what is written about Speed City is the "Black Power" salute by Tommie Smith and John Carlos in the 1968 Olympics in Mexico City. This book is about how my personal experiences with the men of Speed City taught me about racism in America.

A sample of recent headlines and stories in newspapers ten years into the twenty-first century reads like this: "The Civil Rights Trap," "Race Resentment Racket, An Interracial Tipping

Point," "Huntington man charged with hate crimes," "Race Matters," "Civil Rights leaders decry rally plans," "NAACP Sees Racism in 'Tea party'," and "Racism in Mexico Once Again Rears Its Ugly Head."

Racism is so deeply seated in our culture it pops up from time to time in the most unexpected ways. In 2010, National Basketball Association player LeBron James announced he was leaving the Cleveland Cavaliers to play for the Miami Heat. The Cavaliers owner, Dan Gilbert angrily accused James of quitting in games and betraying his hometown. Well known civil rights activist, Jesse Jackson, reciprocally accused Gilbert of treating James like a runaway plantation slave. Both blacks and whites reacted to this statement. Most people, black or white, did not see the connection between a multi-million dollar pro athlete and a plantation slave.

Months later, when asked if race was involved in the backlash of his decision to leave Cleveland to play for Miami, James responded by saying it was. Here is how it appeared on many internet sites on September 30, 2010 under the headline LeBron James: Race Played Role in "Decision" Backlash.

James appeared on the CNN program *Rick's List* on Wednesday night and the NBA superstar said he believes race was a factor in the negative feedback he received after "The Decision."

CNN correspondent Soledad O'Brien mentioned James' brand and name were "tarnished" because of his decision to leave the Cleveland Cavaliers in such a public fashion and asked if race played a role in the backlash.

"I think so at times," James replied. "It's always, you know, a race factor."

Maverick Carter, a twenty-eight-year-old who is one of James' closest advisers, said race "definitely played a role in some of the stuff coming out of the media, things that were written for sure." These comments set off a flurry of debates on radio talk shows the next day.

Then there is this bizarre comment in a Steve Lopez column from African American reverend and radio show host, Jesse Lee Peterson, who said:

"White Americans need to get over the fear of being called racists. As a result of your fear, we now have the worst president this country has ever experienced. Barack Obama is a liar; he is a racist. White people shouldn't have any qualms about using the 'N' word. Let me just say, to free you up, that word don't mean anything to black people because if it did, they would stop saying it and the word would fade away. It's just another way of controlling white Americans, but get over your fear." [1]

During his run for President and since his election there has been a string of racially tinged controversies aimed at President Obama. He graciously never responds but they still offend those who feel demeaned because of their ethnic background. One example was during the presidential campaign, an inland empire, Calif. Republican women's group sent out a newsletter depicting Obama surrounded by ribs, fried chicken and watermelon. And there was the *New York Post* controversy with the cops shooting a chimpanzee and referring to the stimulus package.

Another illustration was an email sent out by Los Alamitos, CA Mayor Dean Grose that depicted the White House front lawn as a watermelon patch. A black woman was one of the recipients. Grose thought the cartoon was light hearted humor, the female recipient was offended. He resigned from office over the email but remains involved in local Republican politics, running again for the City Council a year later.

---

1 Steve Lopez, "Beverly Hills Tea Party' is a rootin', tootin' affair." *Los Angeles Times*, September 29, 2010, 2.

The Republican Party endorsed him in his new run for office. *Orange County Register* columnists Frank Mickadeit wrote about the cartoon and the Republican Party's endorsement of Grose as a candidate, calling it bad judgment. The topic of racism heated up even more with the comments by Walter Myers, Vice Chairman for the Ethnic Communities Committee of the Orange County G.O.P. at a Black Chamber of Commerce Dinner attended by Grose. Here is how Myers weighed in on the flap:

"I'm black, and I know Dean. You idiots on this trail and the idiot who wrote this article don't know what racism is because you have never experienced it. I have. A white man would only send a black woman the cartoon that Dean did because he was making some light humor. I wouldn't have been offended in the slightest.

"White guilt is one of the most pathetic, disingenuous, and destructive things I have ever seen in life. You're worse than the white racists I encountered when working in Atlanta. At least they were honest."

Mickadeit explained his position:

"This idiot writer, however, rejects Myers' implication that because he's black and I'm not… I can't find the watermelon cartoon offensive.

"This idiot writer finds it offensive for the simple reason it implies that Obama is a stupid black man, and only a stupid black man, and that black men can only be stupid. It doesn't imply he's a stupid scholar, lawyer, policy-maker or American— not even that he's a dastardly politician or lousy chief executive. It implies that he is just one thing: a black man—and it uses one of the least-flattering bits of iconography to convey that message. It says that no matter what a black man might achieve, he will never be more than a watermelon-eating pickaninny. The

---

2 Frank Mickadeit, "Black vs. white ('idiot') on racism." *O.C. Register,* September 30, 2010, Local 2.

cartoon is racist on its face."²

I agree, but did you follow that? A Black politician is criticizing a white columnist for criticizing a white mayor for sending out an email with a racist cartoon about our black President. The white columnist concludes his article by criticizing the black politician for his lack of offense at the racist cartoon. The issue of racism still goes round and round.

Next you have a Latino news reporter calling a Jewish TV comedian a "bigot" and accusing a major network of racism and prejudice.

In October 2010, CNN fired newscaster Rick Sanchez, the host of CNN's *Rick's List* for calling Jon Stewart of *The Daily Show* a bigot with the suggestion that Jews run CNN and all the other networks. Previous to this, Sanchez had called President Obama *"a cotton picking President,"* an obvious reference to the slave days. In Sanchez's mind, racism and prejudice stunted his career as a news anchor, saying, *"An anchor is what you give to high-profile white guys."* He says this illustrates that racism exists *"not just (from the right), but also from elite, North-east establishment liberals."* He accuses these liberals of being condescending to him because he is Latino. Sanchez also complained that Stewart had criticized him many times on the "Daily Show" and had called him a "total meathead."

The next week, Stewart did a humorous rebuttal of what Sanchez had said, but with a serious twist. He replayed a segment of a previous Sanchez show where he condemned racism and intolerance in any form.

"On October 4th, I had a very good conversation with Jon Stewart," Sanchez's statement said, *"and I had the opportunity to apologize for my inartful comments from last week. I sincerely extend this apology to anyone else whom I may have offended.*

"As Jon was kind enough to note in his show Monday night,

I am very much opposed to hate and intolerance, in any form, and I have frequently spoken out against prejudice. Despite what my tired and mangled words may have implied, they were never intended to suggest any sort of narrow-mindedness and should never have been made."[3]

"Huntington man charged with hate crimes" read the headline in *The Orange County Register* on Tuesday, Oct. 5, 2010. "A Huntington Beach California man has been charged with hate crimes on accusations that he yelled racial slurs at a black woman and punched her white friend." According to the Orange County District Attorney, the man was playing loud, racist music with explicit anti-black lyrics. He drove his vehicle close to a store where the black woman was shopping and turned up the volume. Later he yelled more racial slurs, stating that interracial relationships were wrong. When the woman's white friend intervened, the yeller punched him in the face and kicked him before fleeing.[4]

These are just a sampling of the existence of racism in our contemporary culture.

---

3 Timothy Mangan, "Sanchez issues apology." *The Orange County Register*, October 7, 2010, News 2

4 Larry Welborn, "Huntington man charges with hate crimes." *The Orange County Register*, October 5, 2010, Local 2.

Introduction

While a student at San Jose State and as a member of it's track team in the late '60s, I had a desire to understand prejudice and racism. I was recruited from Palomar Junior College in San Diego County and given a track scholarship to run for the Spartans, not as a sprinter but as a miler. Without lightning speed, I did not enhance the image of "Speed City." Although I was not a fast sprinter or a world-class athlete, I had a front row seat watching some of the most dramatic events in the history of track and field.

The issue of racism is much broader than black versus white. Every ethnic group has problems. Someone hates them or attacks them because of their race, color or ethnicity. I have seen and had exposure to several forms of racism on an everyday basis; however, these accounts revisit a specific time in my life with a special focus on white racists' attitudes against blacks during the Civil Rights Movement of the '60s.

Being white and having been reared in a small town in California with no African Americans did not prepare me for a multi-cultural world. I had only limited exposure to the hate minorities encountered in American culture. My time spent at San Jose State University changed all of that.

In high school I read the book *Black Like Me*. Set in 1959, John Howard Griffin, a white man in the south, actually dyed his skin black and shaved his head. His mission was to answer this question, "What is it like, really like, to be a Negro in the South today?" He set out to personally discover what he called the "night side" of American life. His true story, written in 1960, documents the racism he experienced firsthand. He was yelled at, spit upon, threatened with death and generally treated like he was worthless. The prejudice he experienced was worse than he had imagined. This book had an effect on me that would come into play years later.

The late 1960s were a time of major transition in American culture—for society at large, and for college students in particular. The Viet Nam War, the peace movement, Students for a Democratic Society, the hippies and Black Power were all influencing America. Debates were going on everywhere: Were you for the war or against it? Was Nixon the right man for president or should he step down? Were you going to join the thousands of pot smokers or reject marijuana? Could you truly say that "Black is Beautiful," or was that beyond you?

For the black track athlete in particular, the late '60s was an especially significant and turbulent time. Until that time, most successful and popular black athletes, with Muhammad Ali being the exception, did not speak out about social issues or racial inequality. But in San Jose, some of the fastest and most famous track athletes in the United States became leaders in the Civil Rights movement. They became catalysts for social change. These Speed City athletes were key players in speaking out against the hate faced by black Americans everywhere in the country. They were also some of the first to be called "Black Athletes" as opposed to the common term of "Negro Athlete."

When I arrived at San Jose State in the fall of 1967, I met an incredible man named Lee Evans. Evans was one of Speed City's best athletes. The next year, in 1968 at the Mexico City Olympics, he would set the world record of 43.8 in the 400-meter dash that would last for twenty years and win a gold medal. He would win a second gold medal in the 4 x 400 relay. Through my relationship with Evans and other black athletes of Speed City, including Smith and Carlos, I learned about the fight against racism and racial inequality.

I do not assume that I learned everything there is to know about racism, but I did see firsthand the hate and prejudice Lee Evans experienced and what it meant to be "Black like Lee." To some, "Black Like Lee" may sound funny, but his views on racism were unusual and unexpected. The way he handled the hatred toward him so impressed me I still talk about it, more than forty years later. The overt and subtle forms of racism Lee endured forced me to face my own unconscious, subtle forms of prejudice.

His attitudes are not unique to him nor do I suggest I have a deep understanding of the bigger picture of racism; however, I met a man who allowed me to see how he dealt with both blatant and subtle forms of racism. The stories define the essence of my friendship with Evans and his attitude toward racism.

In describing my relationships with Evans and other black athletes I run the risk of being misunderstood by both the black and white reader. Some blacks may view me as a racist for even attempting, as a white man, to deal with the topic of racism. The white reader may disagree with my position on the "Black Power" salute at the '68 Games, casting it in a positive light. My white peers who hated the "Black Power" salute at the '68 Olympics still hate it and after reading this book will most likely not change their opinion.

Evans is an honorable man and I will be forever grateful to him for helping me in my understanding of the depth of the problems the African Americans faced in the '60s. Smith and Carlos' motive for demonstrating on the victory stand in Mexico City by bowing their head and raising a black gloved, clenched fist during the national anthem was out of love for their country, not hate. Maybe now they can be viewed as positive role models in the Civil Rights Movement and not as angry militants and villains.

The year before the 1968 Olympics, Evans and Smith were interviewed about the possibility of a boycott by the Negro track athlete. There was no boycott, but you can see the sincerity of their desire to use their talents to address the ongoing civil rights violations present in the U.S. and what led to the "Black Power" salute.

"I think Negroes are realizing that the white man doesn't go by his own rules, such as in civil rights. To the extent that I think things would be different for the American Negro by 1972, I am willing to consider boycotting. We are men first and athletes second. Professional athletes are even quitting now because of prejudice," said Evans.

"There have been a lot of marches, protests and sit-ins on the situation of Negro ostracism in the U.S. And I don't think that this boycott of the Olympics would stop the problem, but I think people will see that we will not sit on our haunches and take this sort of stuff. We are a race of proud people and want to be treated as such. Our goal would not be to just improve conditions for ourselves and teammates, but to improve things for the entire Negro community," said Smith.[5] (The entire interview can be read in Appendix 1.)

Evans, Smith and Carlos deeply love the United States and the freedom it represents along with the principles the nation was founded on. Their desire then and now is to see all men and women enjoy what the United States has to offer. The "Black Power" salute should be renamed the "Freedom Salute."

---

5 Dick Drake, "In their own words." Track & Field News, Mountain View, CA. November 1967.

Chapter One

A seat on a subway

New York City: 1953

My first encounter with the issue of black versus white came when I was five years old. My father, an orthodontist, was president of the local Kiwanis Club. He took the entire family to the annual Kiwanis national convention in New York City. I have vivid memories of riding subways, walking in large parks, dropping things out of the third story window of our host's apartment and touring an NBC studio. In the studio, tourists were shown how this new technology called television worked. I stayed in one room and my sisters went into another room and I could see them on a grainy, black and white TV monitor. An amazing new technology.

It was on one of our subway rides that I had an experience that gave me my first awareness that there was an issue between blacks and whites. It was minor incident, but I have a very clear memory of it.

I was taught that when a woman entered a room and you were seated, the polite thing to do was to get up and offer her your seat.

At age five, I was not aware of any issues associated with race or color. I only saw male and female. The subway was crowded and many people were standing and holding on to dangling straps to keep their balance. My family, minus Dad, was seated and I was on the aisle.

At one stop, a black woman boarded. She was carrying several packages from a shopping trip to the grocery store. She looked tired and her slightly overweight frame sagged when she surveyed the scene to see that no seats were available.

Instinctively, I rose and offered her my seat. You would have thought I cured cancer by her reaction. She began to exclaim to everyone around at her amazement that a little "white" boy gave up his seat for her. It was Christmas morning. It was the reaction you might get when you give someone the best birthday present ever.

Her reaction did not stop. She continued to shake her head in amazement and rehash what had happened. I heard the words "white boy" over and over. I was not sure why my giving up my seat was an issue, but it seemed important to her. To me, it had nothing to do with me being white and her black. It was about common courtesy. I am not sure where I learned this, but all I saw was that she was a woman whom needed a seat.

My mother must have explained to me why this was a big deal. There were most likely other men, both black and white seated in that car, but none were motivated to give up their seat.

I imagine if this had happened in Birmingham or Atlanta, it may have been even a bigger deal, possibly causing tension between the whites and the blacks on the subway. But in 1953, it was not an expectation that a black woman would be treated with common courtesy. When it did happen, it was a memorable event for her. Maybe she had moved to New York after being raised in the South. If she had, she lived with and understood the Jim Crow laws and how they applied to public transportation. One source gives this information about Jim Crow laws.

The Jim Crow laws were state and local laws in the United States mandating racial segregation in all public facilities, with a supposedly "separate but equal" status for black Americans.

In reality, this led to treatment and accommodations that were usually inferior to those provided for white Americans.

Some examples of Jim Crow laws are the segregation of public schools, public places and public transportation, and the segregation of restrooms, restaurants and drinking fountains for whites and blacks. The U.S. military was also segregated. State-sponsored school segregation in most Southern states was declared unconstitutional by the Supreme Court of the United States in 1954 in Brown v. Board of Education. The origin of the phrase "Jim Crow" has often been attributed to "Jump Jim Crow", a song-and-dance caricature of African Americans performed by white actor Thomas D. Rice in blackface, which first surfaced in 1832. "Jim Crow" had become a pejorative expression meaning "African American" and the laws of racial segregation became known as Jim Crow laws.[6]

The uneasy tension which existed between Negroes and whites is described in *Black Like Me*. The scene he describes here is in New Orleans and early on in his experiment.

"When I left him (his Negro friend who shined shoes) I caught the bus into town, choosing a seat halfway to the rear. As we neared Canal, the car began to fill with whites. Unless they could find a place to themselves or beside another white, they stood in the aisle.

"A middle-aged woman with stringy gray hair stood near my seat. She wore a clean but faded print house dress that was hoisted to one side as she clung to an overhead pendant support. Her face looked tired and I felt uncomfortable. As she staggered with the bus's movement my lack of gallantry tormented me. I half rose from my seat to give it to her, but Negroes behind me frowned disapproval. I realized I was 'going against the race' and the subtle tug-of-war became instantly clear. If the whites

---

6 Woodward, C. Vann, The Strange Career of Jim Crow (New York: Oxford Press, 2002), 7.

would not sit with us, let them stand. When they became tired enough or uncomfortable enough, they would eventually take seats beside us, and soon see that it was not so poisonous after all. But to give them your seat was to let them win. I slumped back under the intensity of their stares.

"But my movement had attracted the white woman's attention. For an instant our eyes met. I felt sympathy for her and thought I detected sympathy in her glance. The exchange blurred the barriers of race (so new to me) long enough for me to smile and vaguely indicate the empty seat beside me, letting her know she was welcome to accept it.

"Her blue eyes, so pale before, sharpened and she spat out, 'What're you looking at me like that for?'

"I felt myself flush. Other white passengers craned to look at me. The silent onrush of hostility frightened me.

"'I'm sorry,' I said, staring at my knees. 'I'm not from here.'

"'They're getting sassier every day,' she said loudly. Another woman agreed and the two fell into conversation.

"My flesh prickled with shame, for I knew the Negroes rightly resented me for attracting such unfavorable attention."

Later in that same chapter, he describes a poster he saw hanging on a wall that got his attention.[7]

DESEGREGATE THE BUSES WITH THIS 7 POINT PROGRAM

1. Pray for guidance.

2. Be courteous and friendly.

3. Be neat and clean.

4. Avoid loud talk.

5. Do not argue.

6. Report incidents immediately.

7. Overcome evil with good.

Sponsored by the Interdenominational Ministerial Alliance.[8]

In reflection, I now understand why my giving up my seat was a big deal. I am saddened that it was, but it was my first exposure to the realities of black vs. white. I am thankful that I was not told to stay in my seat.

---

7 John Howard Griffin, (New York: Signet Books, 1960), 24-25.

8 Ibid, 25-26.

Chapter Two

The Old Brick Church

Escondido, California, 1962

Next door to our family home was an unused Catholic Church first built in the early1900s. A newer building had been built about eight blocks away, leaving this classic red brick church with a bell tower sitting empty. The church's bell tower, still with its bell was an easy target for me and my prankster friends. We would sneak in through a broken window and hang on the rope attached to the bell moving it up and down. The ringing could be heard in the neighborhoods around the church.

The bell ringing would bring out the priests and nuns living next to the old church. We would scramble away and hide, thinking they had no idea who was doing the ringing. Of course they did, but were benevolent and did not punish us.

In 1962, the Parish authorities decided to tear down the church. It was interesting to watch the walls come tumbling down with the aid of a tractor and long steel cables. I assumed that the bricks would be hauled off in dump trucks to the local landfill. What I didn't know was used brick was a valuable commodity in that day, so rather than just hauling the bricks off to the local landfill, the church leadership decided to salvage the bricks.

Instead of dump trucks hauling off bricks, I saw palettes of nicely cleaned bricks stacking up. I was curious how they were getting cleaned and stacked, so I wandered over to the church property to see what was going on. It was then I learned the bricks were being salvaged by knocking the old cement free from each brick. The Priests had hired one man to clean the bricks, thousands of bricks by my estimation. The man they hired would sit in a pile of bricks and with a hand–held hatchet he would remove the cement from each brick. One by one he stacked the cleaned bricks on a pallet.

As I approached the man working on the bricks, several things stood out to me. First thing I noticed was that he was a Negro. The second thing was that he appeared to be very comfortable in a low squatted stance while he deftly cleaned each brick. I was impressed with how fast he could pick up a brick in his left hand and in four simple strokes with his small hatchet, clean off the old cement and stack the brick on the palette. Thirdly, he was friendly and welcomed me into his work space. This started a friendship that I enjoyed for the next four months. Many days I would go over and visit with him while he cleaned the bricks. Occasionally he would let me try cleaning a brick or two, but I did not have the skill he did. He worked seven days a week, rain or shine.

During the colder days, he would have a small fire burning for warmth. On the rainy days, he would work under a tarp strung up to function as a tent. He didn't mind that I would sit near him and ask questions about his life, and chat about sports and current events. Through our conversations, I discovered that he was an educated and well-read man. My biggest questions were about how he got there and why he was doing this. He explained work was hard to find, so he left his family in Los Angles to earn what he could doing this painstaking back-breaking brick cleaning job. I don't remember the exact amount he was being paid, but it was not much, maybe less than a nickel a brick. As a teenager, I was both impressed and depressed at what I was seeing. This man was working very hard for very little but appeared happy.

I eventually learned that he ate his meals and spent most nights right there among the bricks, sleeping on a cot under a tarp. He would cook his meals, usually canned beans, with a camp stove. It wasn't only for economic reasons he stayed on the job site. The main reason he stayed was because he faced a hostile environment when he left the security of his mini brickyard. He shared with me an encounter he had with some young men on the street right near the job site. An encounter that was ugly and racist. I was saddened to hear his story and to realize that our town was not friendly to Negroes.

One day while this nice man walking back to his brickyard with two bags of groceries, a car of young men drove by and tossed a large chunk of wood at him. To protect himself, he had to drop the bags and catch the object. Due to the speed of the car and the size of the object, it knocked him over backwards, spilling his groceries, breaking the eggs and spilling his milk. He had a good-sized bump on the back of his head. Still ringing in his ears were the racial slurs that were yelled along with "Get out of town, N-----!"

I was shocked. How could this be happening in a small town in Southern California? Who were these young men and why would they do this? He survived and was very philosophical about this blatant act of hatred. He took the incident in stride, having learned to live with racism as a reality of life. Eventually his work was done and he moved on. I do not remember his name but I remember his character, and it was impressive.

In retrospect, I was impressed with the work ethic he displayed. I could not imagine myself, or anyone I knew, working as hard as he did for as little as he was paid. I also could not imagine him not being bitter and angry from the incident that he told me about. I was puzzled that anyone would hate this man. Did skin color really matter that much? Why was he a threat to our community?

My encounter with this man made an impression on me that seemed to be different than what I was hearing from the culture around me. The general stereotype being portrayed of "Negroes" was that they were uneducated and lazy. Also I had the impression they did not like white people. This impression about not liking white people was made when I was twelve or thirteen playing baseball on a Boys Club team. The coaches arranged for a road trip to play teams in Los Angeles, San Bernardino and Riverside.

Our first stop was in South Los Angeles to play an all black team. We spent the night in the club gym and played the game the next day. Our coaches warned us not to leave the property and wander off into the streets around the club. It was said in such a way to portray danger. One team member named Steve took it as a challenge and left the property on his own. Steve came off as a tough guy and apparently had a confrontation with some locals. He returned with a bloody nose and a fat lip. In retrospect, I think Steve asked for it by saying something deserving of a smash in the mouth, but at the same time it reinforced the feeling that blacks did not like whites.

Much of what I knew or felt about Negroes came from watching television. Movies and TV shows perpetuated less than flattering images of blacks. In the early days of television programming, a black could be either a silly maid or a chauffeur. A TV show that I remember watching was called *Amos and Andy*. The show started as a radio program in the late 1920s with two white men speaking like black men. Eventually *Amos and Andy* became a minstrel show with white men performing in black face, a popular way to portray blacks at the time. It then evolved into a TV show. The show was popular with both blacks and whites as it was the first and only show with an all black cast.

This show became controversial even though most blacks liked it, according to George Kirby in a 1986 documentary show called *Amos 'n' Andy: Anatomy of a Controversy*. Creating this kind of comedy was the only logical way to get blacks on TV in more important roles, explained Kirby. The re-runs of the show were taken off the air permanently in 1966 as a result of a lawsuit filed by the NAACP. NAACP felt the show projected not only a false image, but also a negative image because it was the only image being shown. The NAACP was looking for balance. It became a "casualty of the Civil Rights movement" according to Kirby. Many saw it as comedy and maybe it would have survived if there had been other shows that portrayed blacks as doctors, teachers and policemen.[9]

Looking back on it now, I can see both sides of the argument. It was funny, but at the same time the story lines and the characters were not all that positive as role models. To me the characters of Amos and Andy did not reflect an image of being un-intelligent, just sneaky and conniving. The characters were always looking for a clever way to make a quick buck, even at the expense of their friends. The exaggerated way of speaking was a main focus in the show. To some this may have made them appear unintelligent. Also, the names were a factor in forming images. "Lightning" for the slow moving janitor, "King Fish" for the main character, "Sapphire" for his wife and "Calhoun" for his attorney all fed the image.

In the 1970s, a popular show was *All in the Family*. This primetime satire panned all forms of racism and prejudice exposing the absurdity of hatred based on race, color or creed. Archie Bunker was the archetype of a modern racist. His son-in-law Michael was his foil, the voice of reason, often getting in heated arguments with Archie over his attitudes or racism. In one pointed episode, two of Archie's "Lodge Buddies" were preparing for a variety show the club was going to put on. They were dressed in minstrel-type costumes that included white suits with gold trim and white hats complete with black face. When Michael came home to find the three men rehearsing, the dialog is hilarious with the goal of pointing out the absurdities of racism.

9 Amos and Andy: Anatomy of a Controversy, Directed by Stanley Sheff (1983, USA, PBS).

"I don't believe you guys. You are actually going to put on a minstrel show in this day and age? You ought to get great revues from the Ku Klux Klan. This is the worse kind of bigotry," says Michael with great disgust.

In a moment of sanity, Archie says, *"Wait, the boy is right!"*

Mike is stunned as Archie continues, *"He is absolutely right. This is a bad thing were are doing here. It ain't nice dressing up like that making fun of the colored people. Archie Bunker is not going to get up on the stage and make fun of the people he likes and has admired his entire life."*

Mike is even more stunned and suspicious of Archie's motives. *"You want something?"* he asks in disbelief. In anger Michael says, *"This is ridiculous. You are a pack of racists. How can you be in a lodge like this?"*

Archie continues to agree until his buddies threaten to kick him out of the lodge. Archie reaffirms his love for the lodge brothers. One buddy says *"There ain't nothing wrong with Minstrel Shows."*

Archie then begins to defend minstrel shows to a very disgusted Michael by saying *"Minstrels shows go way back in U.S. history to the carefree days of slavery. Don't look at me like that; that's all a part of your American heresy,"* not realizing he is using the wrong word.

An ever increasing angry Michael says, *"Doesn't it bother you that black people are offended at a show like this?"*

"They ain't going to see it, they ain't allowed in," responds Archie.

That episode ended with Archie not having to be in the show after all as he had to rush off to the hospital for the birth of his first grandchild.[10]

---

10 All in the Family, Birth of the Baby (part 1), CBS Television, (Episode 123, December 15, 1975).

Norman Leer, the creator of *All in the Family,* made great strides in getting America to take a look at the absurdities of racism.

I don't remember any movies specifically that cast blacks in a negative light, only that so few had black actors and actresses portrayed as positive role models. The absence of black leading characters began to change. But it wasn't until 1966 when Harry Belefonte appeared in *I Spy* the movie and in 1967 with Sidney Poitier in *Guess Who's Coming to Dinner?* we started to see blacks in prominent roles. These films were breakthroughs in the area of having a Black in a starring role.

This stereotype of black people did not match with what I experienced interacting with the "brick man." My eyes were opening to the fact that not all was well between the races and that my hometown was not the pristine place many thought it was.

Chapter Three

Do You Know The Way To San Jose?

The Running Route

"5:30 in the morning? Why would I want to get up and run at 5:30 in the morning? Why do you want to get up and run?" This was my response when a friend asked me if I wanted to join him for a pre-dawn run in the fall of 1961.

Fellow high school freshman Jim Ahler was getting up early and running. He wanted to know if I wanted to join him. I was curious. I repeated my questions:

"Why 5:30? Why so early? Where do you run? Why do you run?"

"I am on the cross country team," he said.

"What's the cross country team?" I asked, being totally unfamiliar with the sport.

"We run races against other high schools through the hills and streets around the campus," he said. "And for away meets, we run on hills and streets around their campuses."

"How long is a race?"

"Two miles."

"Two miles? That's a long way to run. Do you get sick?" I asked.

"Not anymore. I am in pretty good shape. I have been running for nearly two months. The cross country coach encouraged everyone on the team to get in extra training by running in the morning. After school is our main workout," he explained.

"How far do you run? Where do you run? Isn't it dark?," I asked.

"Three miles. Maybe sometimes five miles. I leave my house and run over to Juniper Street, you know, just through our neighborhoods. Sometimes I go all the way downtown to Grand Avenue," he explained, "but mostly I stay around here. A couple of times I have run as far south as 17th street."

It was not for the joy of running that got me up the next morning. It was more out of curiosity about what he described as an intriguing adventure, running through the dark streets before most people were awake. He described playing a kind of hide and seek game with the milk delivery truck, the paper man, street sweepers and a few early morning commuters.

Well, the first morning came and I was half asleep and a little nervous. I had everything laid out the night before, but I did not tell my parents about this new adventure. I was afraid they would put the kibosh on me running around in the dark. It was late in October so the air was cool, cold enough I needed to wear sweat pants under my jeans, a sweatshirt with a hood and gloves, at least I thought. After getting bundled up and pulling on my converse basketball shoes, I was ready to go. My father was an early riser so he was already up reading the paper. Not wanting to have him know what I was doing I exited through the outside door of my bedroom.

The cool fresh air rousted me out of my stupor as I stumbled in the dark up the road out to Ninth street behind our house. I jogged down to the corner where Ahler said he would meet me. Sure enough, off in the distance I could see him jogging up the street toward me. He laughed when he saw how I was dressed. He knew it wasn't that cold out and I was over dressed. He was wearing a pair of sweatpants and a sweatshirt with no hood. He didn't even have gloves on.

"You will be peeling off those gloves and sweatshirt in about a mile," he conjectured.

Sure enough, the running heated me up to the point where I had to take off the gloves and hooded sweatshirt. After about two miles I wished I could take off the sweatpants, but that would have required me removing my jeans.

At one point a policeman drove by, causing Ahler and me to hide behind a parked car. This cat and mouse game with the police made this into an even bigger adventure. I don't know why we hid, but thinking we were getting away with something made it fun. I was hooked on the morning runs. So the next morning I pulled on my Levis, sweatshirt, and shoes and went for my second run, minus gloves, hood and sweatpants.

This was kind of a false start for my interest in running. In September, I had tried out for freshman football and failed, throwing my back out and becoming ill after the first week of tryouts. I missed school for the next two weeks, making me realize football was not for me. It was later in the fall when Ahler, also a non-footballer, asked me to join him for the early morning runs.

By now, cross country season was nearly over, but I joined the team anyhow. There was just two weeks left in the season. I started running after school with the team, but never had the chance to compete in a meet. During this two-week period I began to sense that I could run as well as anyone, but because I was late joining the team the coach did not let me run in the last meet of the season. As I watched from the sidelines, something inside me told me that I could have won that race.

I soon put running behind me and forgot the feelings I had about winning the last race of the season. I stopped the morning runs also, feeling a little bitter toward the coach for not letting me run in the final meet. The next spring, I tried out for the freshman baseball team. The coach let me stay on the team more out of sympathy than any skills I brought to the team. In fact, the only time I got into a game was when my presence could not influence the outcome one way or the other. I was on the team more for comic relief, always clowning around during bus rides and in the dugout during the games. But I missed an obvious clue about my true athletic ability during the spring.

While playing baseball, my class schedule did not permit me to have physical education at the end of the day, like all the other players. One other player, Mike Jessen, was in the same situation. Not having 7th period P.E. required that Jessen and I meet the team late for practice. The biggest problem was the practice field was one and a half miles away from the school and the team bus was not available for us late starters. To get there, Jessen and I had to run to the practice in our baseball cleats, glove in hand and wearing our heavy wool uniforms.

It was an easy task for me. It never occurred to me that getting there should have been more of a problem than it ever was for me. I could run the entire mile and a half without tiring or losing my breath. Jessen, on the other hand, was always yelling at me to slow down and wait for him. I should have been on the track team, but I knew nothing about track and my love for baseball blinded me to my ability to run.

By the end of the season, my hopes of getting a coveted freshman athletic letter were dashed when I was the only player not to get one. That really hurt. Getting a letter meant you could buy a letterman's jacket and join an exclusive group on campus.

At that point, I was done with sports! Most of my friends were wearing letterman jackets, proudly displaying the letter they won during the year participating in one of a number of sports. I felt left out. I was on the outside looking in because I could not be part of the group wearing the orange and black jackets of our school colors.

It was the next fall that I accidentally found my niche in sports and earned something better than a freshman letter—a varsity letter as a sophomore. During 2nd period P.E. class, our teacher had all the students run two miles every day. One day when I finished the run and stood by the teacher, he asked me a question.

"Do you see what is going on here?"

"No, what do you mean?"

"You are here with me and where is the next runner?" He pointed out the next runner, a good half mile from the finish.

"Yeah, so what?" I answered in a somewhat disinterested manner.

"You should be on the cross country team," he responded.

"No thanks, I tried sports last year and things didn't work out very well," I said, still hurting from being the only baseball player not to get a letter and not being allowed to run the race I thought I could have won.

"Yes, but you should reconsider. You obviously can run better than most students," he argued.

"The only way I would run is if you can get me 7th period P.E.," I said, "I don't want to come out late everyday and miss part of the practice."

The coach spoke to the right people and the change was made. I joined the cross country team without really knowing what was involved, having very little exposure to the sport. After several weeks of practice and two meets, I was running for the Varsity squad and well on my way to getting a varsity letter. I finished the year as the team's second best runner, behind junior Pete Vargas. This allowed me to buy both a letterman's jacket and a letterman's sweater with the coveted three stripes, two of which remained covered. Each successive year, as you earned another varsity letter, you could uncover another stripe. My running career was under way and I wore my Letter with pride. My wounded pride was healed. Who needed a freshman letter? Not me. I had moved ahead of my athletic classmates, none of who had won a varsity letter as sophomores.

Although I had success in cross country, it was during track season my junior year when I started running the mile. With no experience, I ran 4:45 the very first time I tried and never ran slower than that the next 6 years. I learned a lot about competition and about running the mile, especially when the outcome of many of our meets in high school depended on me winning the mile. I discovered I loved it.

In high school, I lowered my mile time to 4:19.2 and in junior college to 4:09.9. It was in Junior College, under first year coach Larry Knuth, that my running skills really improved. As a result, I gained the attention of a number of four-year schools and was offered several scholarships. I was ready to move to the next level of competition. I accepted San Jose State's offer. Even though my mile time was not world class, it was good enough to give me the opportunity to compete along with world class athletes.

When I started running with Jim Ahler that morning in 1961, I had no idea running would eventually lead me to so many special life experiences. At San Jose, I was going to be teammates with some of the world's best track athletes. (To read more about my running experiences, turn to Appendix 8.)

Chapter Four

Lee, will you help me?

By 1967, Lee Evans' success on the track was well documented. While running for Overfelt High School in San Jose, California, Evans was undefeated in his high school career, improving his 440-yard time from 48.2 in 1964 to 46.9 in 1965. As a college freshman, he attended San Jose City College and won his first AAU championship in 440 yards in 1966. He won the first two of his four AAU titles by 1967. Starting his sophomore year of college, he enrolled at San Jose State, where he was coached by Hall of Fame inductee Lloyd (Bud) Winter.

I was fully aware of Evans' track success. I saw him run at the West Coast Relays in Fresno Calif. and the California Relays in Modesto Calif. during the previous two years while I was in junior college. But it was in the big International meets that made him a super star in the track and field world. I watched him win the 400 meter dash in 45.2 and run a leg in the 1600 meter relay in the International Games in 1966 in the Los Angeles Coliseum. This was Lee's first world record performance, with this relay team being the first to ever break three minutes, running 2:59.6. He won the 400 meter dash again the next year at the USA-Commonwealth Games, again at the Los Angeles Coliseum. He teamed with Tommie Smith and two others to win the 1600 meter relay by one-tenth of a second against a British Commonwealth all-star team. In 1967 at the West Coast Relays, he helped set the world record in the 4 X 220 yard relay of 1:22.1.

I remember clearly the time and place I first met and shook hands with Lee Evans. It was in Coach Bud Winter's office. Winter's office was a favorite gathering place for the track team, so it was there I first was formally introduced to Evans. To say I was in awe may be an exaggeration, but I definitely knew I was meeting someone very special.

I had never met or been friends with a well-known and successful athlete with world records, I did not know what to expect. Because of his success and accomplishments, I thought maybe he would have a big ego or not care to hang around athletes of lesser ability. I quickly discovered the opposite was true. His humility belied his ever-growing fame in the track world. He was friendly and outgoing, the type of person who liked to laugh a lot with a great sense of humor. You could sense immediately he knew how to tease and be teased.

Having been around him in the coach's office and in the locker room at the training facility, I could see Evans was fair minded and unbiased in his acceptance of those around him, black or white. I began to think about my limited exposure to blacks. I realized I had no black friends. I also started thinking about Griffin's book, *Black Like Me*. I had been intrigued by Griffin's actions described in the book, but I knew very little about the realities of life for Negroes. The idea came to me that I would ask Lee to help me learn something about his life and mine. Evans' friendliness, camaraderie, and "esprit de corps" gave me the confidence to ask him for the help I was looking for.

So in the fall of 1967 I approached Evans in the hallway outside Winter's office. I told him I had something serious to talk to him about. At first he laughed because we were usually joking around about something, so he was waiting for the punch line.

"No joke, I am being serious now," I said as we sat on a short flight of stairs leading to the basketball gym. "Lee, I am from a small town in San Diego County. I did not grow up with any African Americans. (I believe at the time I used the word Negroes, which was acceptable.) Still unsure if there was a punch line coming he wryly smiled and said, "Yeah, so what?"

He began to sense I was serious. I said, "I do not know what life is like for you. I would like to have you show me how prejudice and racism affects your life on a daily basis. Will you help me?"

"Sure, Jim, but why do you want to do this?" he asked.

"I want to understand, in the best way I can as a white man, the prejudice you deal with on a daily basis. I want to see firsthand and learn about racism," I explained. "I want to discover any attitudes of racism or prejudice in me so that I can rid myself of them."

"You are serious!" he responded. Up to this point most of our conversations were light hearted and filled with one-line jokes and gentle chiding. He could see I was serious, but maybe he was still a little skeptical of this request. "Tell me again what you want me to do and why."

"I know very little about how racism affects you and all Negroes on a daily basis. I want to learn about the realities of racism," I offered. "I want to discover my personal feelings about racism. "Did the way my parents raise me create within me bad attitudes toward Negroes and other minorities? If so, I want to rid myself of them." I continued with "I want to know if racism is just a perception minorities have, as some of my white friends have said, or is it real? I have heard that everyone has some prejudice in them. I don't want that to be true of me." I really wanted answers to these questions. Evans obviously said yes. For the next few minutes the light-hearted bantering we were used to ceased while talked about the uniqueness of this request.

"I will help you," Evans responded. "I think we both will

learn something through this."

To my amazement, Evans was the perfect person to ask for help. He appeared to be energized by the idea. For the next two years, he would allow me to look at the personal affronts he suffered and by extension, what all blacks and minorities experienced on a daily basis. I could tell by the smile on his face he was going to enjoy making a white friend from a small town in Southern California aware of the difficulties he and other blacks faced. This was the beginning of a two-year learning experience and lifelong friendship with my mentor, Lee Evans.

I was not sure how he would go about helping me, but Evans was. He knew how he could educate me. He had ideas that would take me into his world to observe both the overt and the subtle forms of racism that were part of his daily life. Getting the answers to my questions was going to be an exciting process. Our friendship moved to a deeper level.

One factor that helped with this project was we both shared the same major, Physical Education. This gave us the opportunity to study together for tests and to work on homework assignments. But the main component was being teammates. The shared camaraderie of going into competition, traveling together, working out, and having a shared vision for a NCAA title all contributed to a relationship of trust. Even though athletically Evans was on a different level than the majority of his teammates, he treated us as peers. His personal success did not make him unapproachable.

My education at San Jose State outside the classroom rivaled what I learned from lectures and books. Evans was teaching me things you could not learn from traditional methods. My new understandings of racial relationships went way beyond academics. I am thankful for the Bachelor of Arts degree I received, but even more thankful for the insights I gained into one of life's most difficult issues.

I learned other things besides racism from Evans—talent was not a substitute for hard work. Dedication went hand in hand with talent. Evans demonstrated he had a strong work ethic. Some might think with the immense talent he had, he would not need to work as hard as others to have success. Nothing could have been further from the truth. I saw it the first time in September of '67.

The fall was cross country season for distance runners. Our distance coach, Ted Banks had us doing long and hard training runs, which was to be expected. What surprised me were the training runs that Coach Winter was putting the sprinters through that fall. Lee and the other sprinters and quarter milers were doing long distance training to build strength. Coach Winter had them on a workout schedule that would culminate in a ten mile run in November.

The goal was to run the ten miles in under seventy minutes. This distance training was designed to build a strong base for the sprint workouts that would come in the spring. Every day, as the cross country team would head out on a run, we would see the sprinters adding a little more distance to their daily run. I had never seen sprinters run long distances or work as hard as they did. The hard work paid off for them the following spring.

Even though physically and athletically we were very different, Evans and I found a common bond through being teammates, but more deeply through our mutual desire to understand prejudice and racism.

Lee was an impressive physical specimen. A little taller than six feet, his muscles were well defined, both in his legs and his upper body. His stomach muscles or abs were so well developed they looked like a washboard. His body fat index must have been below 5 percent. A good index for athletes can range from 6 to 13 percent. His strict training regimen had him below that. In my opinion, he had the perfect build for a 400-meter runner.

Evans had an abundance of natural ability, worked hard and kept himself in good shape. His dark skin glistened during his strenuous workouts.

I, on the other hand, did not have a well-chiseled body. I was also a little over six feet tall but did not have any real muscle definition in my arms or legs and my stomach was more like a doughboy's. At twenty years of age I was already battling a weight problem. To start with, I was large for a distance runner compared to most other runners. Many were well under six foot and 145 to 150 pounds. My best running weight was 175 pounds. The summer before moving to San Jose, I injured my back and was unable to run for about a month. During that time, I gained thirty pounds and arrived at San Jose weighing 205. Coach Ted Banks did not recognize me the day I arrived that fall. By November, Banks had made sure my weight was back under control.

Although we were very different physically and not equals athletically, we had a great friendship. I was learning that even great athletes needed friends, not just adoring fans. I always felt comfortable being with Lee, knowing our friendship was unconditional. He was fun to be with, always ready to make a joke or laugh at one of mine, never taking himself too serious.

Chapter Five

The First Lesson

Spring 1968

In the fall of 1967, Evans and I took time to get to know each other as friends. There were no major lessons being taught. Evans was serious about helping me see into his world, but was letting our friendship grow first. I was enjoying the casual nature of our friendship and there was no sense of urgency to show me the ugly side of racism. Even so, Evans was encouraging me to stick with him and I would learn.

By the spring of 1968 things picked up. On a Sunday, I accompanied Evans, his wife Linda and toddler son Keith to church in East San Jose. The church congregation was all African Americans and the singing was done a cappella. This in itself was a great cultural and inspirational experience. It was obvious to me this group loved God and loved to sing about Him.

After church, Evans dropped me off at my apartment and said that he and his family would be back in thirty minutes and said we were going on a picnic.

"A picnic? How is this going to teach me about what it is like to be black?" I countered.

"Trust me. Be ready in thirty minutes," he responded with assurance.

Confused, I changed into Bermuda shorts, a t-shirt and my

running shoes, since he suggested we would also work out after lunch with a short run. In the back seat of the car was a large picnic basket. We started to drive.

"Where are we going for the picnic?" I asked.

"Just wait. You will see."

San Jose is in the middle of Santa Clara Valley. At that time, it had one major north south freeway, the 17 Freeway, as it was known. The 17 connected the beach town of Santa Cruz with the 101 freeway, the main route to San Francisco. As we reached the 17 Freeway, we headed south. Are we going to the beach in Santa Cruz? The mountains? My mind was abuzz with possible destinations.

At the southern end of the Santa Clara Valley is a wealthy community called Los Gatos. Wealthy and white would be more accurate. In Los Gatos is a large park with a lake called Vasona Park. This county park had lots of grassy picnic areas and was a popular spot for families on Sunday afternoons The first thing you notice from the parking lot is a child's play ground with swings and slides. A little further away was the lake with a flock of ducks and men with fishing lines cast out in the water. Scattered around the large lawn areas and edge of the lake were many families having picnics and playing with their children. Even further off in the distance were several sand volleyball and basketball courts filled with energetic players.

We parked and headed to the edge of the lake where we found an open spot. Lee spread out a blanket and we sat down to enjoy the picnic lunch of sandwiches, chips and brownies that Linda had prepared.

About fifteen minutes went by when I asked, "Lee, how is this teaching me anything?" I was a little impatient. I guess I was thinking that a trip to the ghetto areas of the Bay Area would teach me more. I wasn't sure what he was doing.

He said, "Just eat and watch what happens."

"What is going to happen?"

"Just watch."

Sure enough, here came a white man jogging on a well-worn path around the edge of the lake that apparently many joggers and walkers used. I didn't notice anything unusual about him or even give him a second thought until he uttered the most disgusting thing he could. His words shocked me.

As he casually passed by us, he spoke in a very clear voice, "Get out of town N-----!" He didn't appear to go out of his way to give his hateful message to Lee and his family. He hardly broke stride. They were just sitting near his normal jogging path. I could not believe I was hearing this in 1968 in California.

At first, I doubted I heard what I heard. But there was no doubt.

Did he just say what I thought he said? I looked at Evans and his family thinking they would be upset. He looked back with a knowing look that said to me, "this is what we deal with."

Evans said, "You wanted to know what my world is like, didn't you?"

I said, "Yes, but did that really just happen?"

"Of course it did," Evans said with a slight smile on his face indicating he was amused by my shock and naiveté.

It did happen and it was shocking to me. It wasn't shocking to Lee and Linda. They knew it was coming. It had happened many times before. Evans knew I would see racism in action if we picnicked at this beautiful park in Los Gatos.

I was disgusted. This man had no idea who he was talking to. He did not see this was one of the world's greatest 400-meter runners, an intelligent college student, a loving husband and father. He just saw a black man and his family invading his white world.

But worse yet, he did not see him as a fellow human being worthy of his respect. His hatred for blacks and, I imagine, all minorities overrode any sense of civility. I knew hateful and bigoted people existed in the world, but this was my first personal encounter with one.

I was confused. What would possess this man to act this way? How come he felt this was his park? That this park was for whites only? I was angry inside. Why didn't I run after the man, or yell at him or do something. I think I was too stunned, but I also was taking my cues from Lee and Linda. Why didn't they react in anger? Why didn't Evans defend his family's honor? I think they were showing me how they handled the offensive and idiotic behavior of hateful and immature people.

Although to me, this was eye opening, to Lee and Linda Evans, it was normal. They did not react in any way to dignify the man's comment. They had matured to the point where they realized that this was not their problem, but this white man's. In spite of this overt sign of hatred, we did not leave. We stayed and enjoyed the day. Lee and I went for a short training run around the park, leaving Linda to entertain Keith in the children's play area with a swing set and a slide.

There were no further incidents of overt racism that day. Lesson one was over. We said very little on the ride home. I think Lee and Linda were giving me time to emotionally and intellectually process this act of overt hatred.

Chapter Six

"Good job, Lee!"

A San Jose Classroom

I soon learned not all racism is overt. Some racism is very subtle and not intended to be mean or hurtful. Things can be said and done that reveal inner prejudices someone may not even be aware of. But the subtle forms are just as real as the overt use of the "N-word" to the black American.

This lesson was one of the hardest for me to understand. But it spoke to the heart of the issue in regards to my own desire to discover what was really going on inside of me. I came to see that I, along with many white people, had an inborn sense of ethnic superiority that affected the way I viewed others, especially blacks. It is not a hateful attitude, just an underlying one. This feeling of ethnic superiority is usually accompanied by another belief: other ethnic groups are also intellectually inferior to the white person. Again, especially blacks.

Evans and I shared the same major, putting us together in classes. We would study together, encouraging one another to do well. We had a mutual desire to succeed academically. These study sessions began to reveal the feeling I was innately more intelligent than Evans, but it was obvious I wasn't. We just put in the time and worked hard.

One day, the professor handed back a test the class had taken. Evans and I both had the same score, a B plus. The teacher wrote across the top of Evan's paper "Good job, Lee!" Nothing was written on mine. No big deal to me. But to Lee here was a lesson.

He asked me if I saw a problem with the note on his paper. I said no. Should I? He then pointed out to me that this was a subtle form of racism.

"C'mon Lee, how can that be?"

"He was surprised I did that well and he just had to say something. He carries the belief that blacks are inherently stupid and he was surprised that I did so well," he said.

"Aren't you reading a little too much into this?" I asked.

"Then why didn't he write something on your paper?" he asked.

"I don't know. Maybe he likes you and he doesn't like me," I answered.

"You are white. He expected you to do well. No need to write a comment," Evans pointed out.

I did not like this reasoning. I knew people felt this way about blacks, but was this the evidence to prove it? In our relationship, we would encourage one another to challenge each other about our views on various issues that we encountered and discuss them openly and honestly. The grade comment issue was one I felt needed further discussion.

"Lee, I think you are reading way too much into this comment," I countered. "Isn't he just being nice? You should just leave it at that."

"When you see the same thing over and over throughout your life, you are able to spot this subtle form of prejudice," he said. "It is a pattern. He is not hateful or mean; it is just an attitude he carries that comes out in gestures like this."

Wow! This was really hard for me to accept. I struggled with this and we discussed it for several days. At first, I really thought Evans was making a mountain out of a molehill. He was looking for something that wasn't there, seeing prejudice and racism under every rock.

Who was I to say he was wrong. Having never been on the receiving end of racism, I had no experience to back my argument. So as the class went forward, I listened and watched the professor, looking for the subtle signs that would support Evans' argument or reinforce mine.

I liked the professor and felt he was an educated, compassionate man. I did not want to find fault with him and neither did Evans. However, Evans was right. Through his interactions with the class and his comments, you could see that the professor did have an underlying belief that blacks were of inferior intelligence.

What amazed me was that Evans did not blame the man or even hate him for this subtle form of racism because he knew that it was a product of our culture. To be honest, I had to dig deep and admit I carried this attitude to a certain degree myself. I had heard it somewhere in my past. I was learning it wasn't true. It was a lie perpetuated by our white society. Lee was living proof it was a lie. His maturity and positive attitude prevented him from reacting in hatred and resentment.

In Evans' biography, *The Last Protest: Lee Evans in Mexico City*, he talks about life as a public elementary school student in the tiny town of Madera, outside of Fresno, California. Earlier he had told me how seeing the same things over and over his whole life helped him spot the subtle form of prejudice such as the professor's with his "Good job, Lee!" comment. In the third grade he started to notice he and his black classmates were treated differently.

"At the school Lee went to the white kids sat in the front

near the teacher, while Lee and the other two black kids sat in the back. From there Lee had a good view of the whole room. He saw that the white kids didn't get in trouble for the little bits of mischief that got him and his two seatmates in trouble. One time Lee said to the teacher, 'I do not want to sing today,' but the teacher made him do it anyway. But when the white kids said that they did not want to sing, the teacher said nothing and they did not sing.

"This is a small matter to be pulled out and examined, you might say, but the small events are the components of memory, and memory is what makes a person. It comes to this: The young Lee Evans was noticing the way he was being treated. More to the point, he was noticing that he was being treated differently than the white kids. Knowing this, he did not rustle or fight because his nature was quiet. The things he noticed, he noticed for himself. But they were important."[11]

---

11 Frank Murphy, *The Last Protest: Lee Evans in Mexico City* (Wind Sprint Press, 2006), 23.

Chapter Seven

Paddle Foot and Crown Head

One day Evans decided he was going to call me "Paddle Foot." This was because I wore size fifteen shoes. We were good enough friends that he felt comfortable enough to chide me about this unique feature of a guy only six feet one inches tall, 175 pounds and a miler at that. It was a term of endearment.

I asked him what his nickname was. He said "Crown Head." He earned this nickname as a child because his head was larger than most and had a crown shape. So from that day on we would greet each other with "How you doin', Paddle Foot?" "Just fine, how about you Crown Head?"

These were nicknames only used between us. To me there was nothing derogatory in calling him "Crown Head" especially since he gave me permission to call him that. Well, I found out in an unexpected way that other blacks were offended by my calling him by this nickname.

The West Coast Relays in Fresno was one of the biggest meets on the west coast, especially in the '60s. My first time at the relays was in 1966 with our Palomar College team. I was totally amazed at the number of fans that attended this meet as well as the quality of competition. The big deal was that if you won a race, you received a gold watch. Everyone coveted the gold watch. I never won one while running for Palomar College.

My first year at San Jose, I ran the third leg of a distance medley team, three laps or what we called then the 1320. We had a good team and our miler, Pete Santos, ran a 4:07 mile and we won. I got my first gold watch. Inscribed on the face in red letters was West Coast Relays, 1968. I was thrilled. I thought I had won my first watch earlier in the four-man two mile relay. Each runner runs two laps or a half-mile. This race was a headline race with a team from Kansas with Jim Ryun, a team from Villanova with Dave Patrick, BYU and us. Our relay team of Jack Malloy, Paul Myers, Santos and myself had posted the best time in the world the month before at the Santa Barbara Relays at 1:24 in a race against USC. Everyone was anticipating a fast time and maybe even a world record.

I ran the second leg in 1:52 keeping us in contention. The Kansas runners had dropped way back and Kansas with Ryun appeared to be out of contention. Our anchor runner was Santos, primarily a miler. He had us in the lead as the runners started up the backstretch of the last lap. But here came Patrick, an Olympic athlete, and Ryun, a world record holder. The dream of a watch was gone as Santos faded and Patrick held off a charging Ryun at the tape in a time of 7:23.6, a new world best for that year. Ryun ran an incredible leg of 1:46.6 to nearly make up a big deficit.

That night, teams from San Jose State did well and many watches were won. Relay teams from San Jose State also won the 880 yard relay (two laps, each man running 220 yards) and the mile relay (each man running 440 yards). Evans ran the anchor or last leg for each of these races. The mile relay, usually the last event of the night, was one of the most exciting as Evans came from behind to give San Jose the emotional win in a great time. Evans ran a 44.9 440 to edge Larry James of Villanova by seven-tenths of a second. We were so excited we carried him off the track singing "Do you Know the Way to San Jose?" a Dionne Warwick hit in the '60s.

For the trip back to our motel, I was sitting near the back of the team bus. Lee stepped on to the bus and saw me in the back. He yelled out, "How many watches did you win tonight Paddle Foot?" I answered, "One. How many did you win Crown Head?" As he answered "two," the bus fell silent. All eyes were on me. It was like one of those E.F. Hutton ads where everything gets quiet and the words "Crown Head" seemed to hang in the air.

The looks I was getting told me I had said something wrong. I could feel the tension in the air. It was not until that moment that I realized his nickname had racial overtones when used by a white person. Since no one else ever heard us greeting one another, I had no idea it was offensive. It was a very uncomfortable moment for me. I had crossed a line. I had spoken out of turn. I had offended the black athletes on the team. I was nervous and unsure of what to do next.

Quickly Evans made his way to where I was sitting to explain to me what was wrong. In whispered tones he explained calling him "Crown Head" in front of the black athletes or "brothers" was offensive because they didn't understand our relationship. I learned it was more than just a term signifying an ethnic connection, but also of the shared experience of being socially ostracized by whites. The term "Crown Head" was similar to using the "N-word" when used by a white person. He suggested I only use the nickname when we were alone. I readily agreed.

Apparently, those I offended were set at ease when they saw Evans and me having a close and friendly conversation in the back of the bus. I imagine he put the word out that I was not trying to offend, but that our "nicknames" were just part of the relationship he and I had.

After that, I sensed a new openness by all of the blacks on the team toward me. I began to receive invitations to their post-meet parties where we all ate hogs-paws and greens, beans, black-eyed peas, and fried chicken. The food was delicious and I felt privileged to be sharing this time with them. They also would share a hand slap with one another in place of a handshake, similar to the "high-five" popular today. It was a greeting shared by the "brothers" and I usually received a handshake. One day, feeling comfortable enough with my "insider" relationship, I started asking for hand slaps instead of a handshake. I was pleased to be considered "slap worthy."

Being in those social situations game me opportunities to observe other cultural issues unique to blacks. I was fascinated by the various ways the "N-word" was used within the context of black to black. As trust grew between my black teammates and me, I was told more of the insider phrases they used with each other. My black teammates had two kinds of "N-words." At times the word was used in a fun way to tease each other after a track meet. If a guy seemed to be weak and did not fare well in the competition that day, they would refer to him, in a loving and jovial manner, as a "House N-word." The house slave was a man who was not strong enough to work in the fields, to do real work. He was sheltered. An athlete who showed strength by performing well and succeeding, he was called "Field N-word." Being referred to as a "Field N-word" was a badge of honor. To keep the level of intensity up, the N-word was elongated and ended in the "Ah" sound instead of the "R" sound, Nigg-aah. The use of the "N-word" was not limited to house or field, but sometimes it was used as a greeting and as a term of affection, especially the elongated "aah" version.

Something else I observed was the genuine camaraderie between all blacks. The common experience of being black in a "white man's world" was a common denominator all blacks shared with one another. I saw a unique unity as a result of mutual experiences of prejudice and hate most blacks had experienced based on the color of one's skin. Blacks understood the impact of racism in America and the awareness had the effect of creating a strong brotherhood. It didn't matter if a "black brother or sister" had light skin or dark skin, or where they were raised, the "brotherhood" connection was instant.

Another thing I enjoyed about my teammates was the way they spoke to each other. It was common for them to use slang words familiar to them. The words would be said with an accent or cadence that was understandable to my black teammates but not to your average white person. Conversations could be carried on within earshot of someone not in tune with the lingo being used and they would not understand what was being said. It was called "Jive Talk." Jive Talk was panned in the movie *Airplane* when two blacks were using Jive Talk and were interpreted by an unlikely person—an older white woman. The woman was the actress Barbara Billingsley, better known as the mother in *Leave it to Beaver*, a popular 1950s TV sitcom.

But any form of the "N-word" used by a white was never acceptable. I was reminded of this during a workout, a medium speed eight mile run. After Nixon was elected in 1968, the nation was in a time of change and turmoil over the war in Viet Nam, the Civil Rights Movement and a host of other issues. Being from a conservative town and family, I was more of a law and order person. I felt there was a right way to demonstrate and there was a wrong way. The demonstrators using the wrong way needed to be repressed by any means necessary.

During the run, I was having a heated discussion with a fellow white teammate, Andy Vollmer, about this issue. He was tolerant of Civil disobedience as a legitimate form of expression and was a Nixon hater. We were bantering about the riots that were happening across the country at the time and we both had entrenched ourselves in our positions of what was right and what was wrong.

We were on opposite ends of the scale when it came to civil unrest. I took the law and order side and he took the side of the demonstrators, no matter what they were doing to get their point across. Sometimes it was smashing cars, burning buildings and throwing rocks. This generally brought out a strong reaction by riot police, resulting in the beating with sticks of the demonstrators and the use of dogs for crowd control.

After debating the use of force back and forth several times Vollmer said, "So you say 'If the (N-word) needs beating, then beat him.'" I responded in a way that I am not proud of, but I was speaking euphemistically when I said, "Yea, if the (N-word) needs beating, then beat him." I meant the "N-word" to identify a class of demonstrators who did not represent the majority of blacks and had lost their focus. It seemed they were just causing damage, damage to their own communities, with no real aim or purpose.

As the words came out of my mouth, I noticed Larry Walls running next to me. Larry was a very good 400-meter hurdles runner and black. I was chagrined at using the derogatory term. Larry was not happy that we were using the "N-word" the way we were.

"Hey guys, cool it with the "N-word," Walls interjected. "I am right here and I would appreciate if you stopped using the "N-word." Andy and I readily agreed. Fortunately, Walls held many of the same attitudes about prejudice as Evans in that he did not get outwardly angry at us.

Overall, Larry was also cool about it. He understood the argument. He apparently had been listening for some time and somewhat agreed that not all demonstrators were helping the Civil Rights cause. Some by their car burning, rock throwing and looting actions were giving all blacks and anyone in favor of the Civil Rights Movement a bad name. Just because they were black did not justify burning buildings and cars, let alone in the name of advancing the Civil Rights Movement.

Since then I have never used the "N-word" in a flippant or joking way. Although I can never really feel the sting it brings when used by a white against a black, to me it will never lose its distasteful flavor.

Chapter Eight

"Aha"

I felt good, maybe even a little smug, about my new awareness of racism and the "insider" relationships I had with my black teammates. However, one day a deeper truth about myself was revealed at a 7-11 convenience store. I had met many of Evans' friends during my first year at San Jose. Linda was really nice and I always enjoyed being around her. Because I had a girlfriend back in Escondido, we never formally dated, but we did spend time together on several occasions as friends. My relationship with her and changes she was going through revealed to me some deep-seated feelings that I had not come in touch with. My true inner feelings about how blacks should relate to the "white culture" came to the surface.

When I first met Evans, he was still getting his hair cut short on the sides with an attempt to comb it over on the top. A part was cut in to make it look even more like a white haircut. Up until 1967, the Afro was not in style. Although I never really gave hair much thought, it seemed blacks were pressured to make their hair be more like the white culture around them, keeping it cropped short. Women had to make a bigger effort to try and conform to what was perceived as an acceptable hairstyle.

Starting around 1968, the Afro started to come into style. To many whites, a black person growing an Afro seemed more like he or she was making a statement than promoting a new hair style. There was a growing freedom among blacks to embrace what was natural about their bodies rather than to repress it. More importantly, there was a new freedom to show the predominantly white culture that this was a "new day." There was also a steep learning curve for both the "white" and black cultures to understand this "new" look.

To many white people, the Afro became a symbol of rebellion. It made some white people uncomfortable, me included. It was a break from what we were used to. It seemed normal for blacks to continue striving to look, act and fit into white society. Maintaining the status quo, or in other words, keeping the blacks feeling repressed and inferior, was what was important for many white people. This Cultural Revolution affected everyone.

In many ways, the Afro really was a rebellion, a rebellion against an evil and ugly repression which had existed for many years. I could read about Rosa Parks and see freedom marches on TV, but those newsworthy events were not the same as the close personal encounters going on in front of me. I could read about the marches and lunch counter sit-ins in the Southern States and feel anger toward the "white" oppressors, but in reality, I had no clue how hard life was for those who were economically disadvantaged due to race. I was culturally white and about to discover I also had biased feelings toward minorities.

I confronted one of these biases one day. As I was walking out of the 7-11, Linda was walking in. I had not seen her for several months. During that time, she had joined the "revolution" and had changed her look. The attempt to straighten her hair was a thing of the past. She was now sporting a very large Afro. I did not recognize her immediately because she looked so different. But it was not her new hairstyle getting my attention and revealing something about myself.

As we chatted for a few minutes, I noticed a button she had pinned on her blouse and the words on the button shocked me. The message on her button made me feel uncomfortable.

To my surprise it revealed and addressed my inborn prejudice. The words opened my eyes to an ugly truth about myself. Deep inside, I had conformed and accepted the lie "white is right." The three words proudly displayed on her blouse struck at a troubling inner truth, veiled up to now. The truth was I felt comfortable with the cultural status quo for blacks.

The button had a simple message, "Black is Beautiful." This was the very first time I had ever seen or heard this phrase. My thinking was turned upside down. I had been conditioned to think only white is beautiful and normal. I never was aware or sensed I had an inborn bent toward this racist view. In fact, I was priding myself in my efforts to be friends with Evans and other blacks, not realizing even those actions could be interpreted as a form of racism. But the truth was I needed to become aware of and address my true feelings. I had work to do.

Where these inner feelings come from is hard to tell. Being raised in an upper middle class Caucasian culture definitely skews your views toward those different than you. Most of the influence is more subtle than overt. Watching police dogs biting blacks while white policemen beat them on the evening news at events like the Watts Riots, lunch counter sit-ins and desegregation of schools and businesses affect one's view of who is right and who is wrong.

Although my parents were not overtly racist, their complacent attitude about these actions against blacks did affect me. Listening to what the adults around are saying and not saying sinks in and becomes ingrained in you. No matter how hard you try to move away from them, the dormant negative attitudes stay with you.

The "Black is Beautiful" button was an "Aha" moment for me. Now I could see myself for who I really was. If I was serious about culling out any wrong and bias attitudes in me, this was definitely the watershed. I did not change that day and I would have to say that even to this day, I am not completely free of the negativity that came with growing up in the environment I did. However, being aware of these tendencies has helped me be sensitive about the words I use and how I speak about others. My desire is to be positive and loving in my relationships with all of humanity.

After sharing my "Aha" moment with Evans, he continued to point out to me the multiple forms of prejudice he faced. I became more and more aware of the affronts he and other minorities faced. Signs of bias would happen and he would point them out to me, subtle slights that Evans noticed and clearly understood the meaning of, but I was oblivious to. They were forms of racism I was guilty of myself, but never understood how they came across.

One example of the visible signs of bias came when we were riding around the city of San Jose in his car was the double take. If we were driving in a predominately white community and we would pull up to a stop sign behind a car of whites, inevitably the people in the back seat would give a double take look over their shoulder. To me, they may have been looking at his car or just being casual about who was behind them. But to Evans, after seeing it time and time again, it was the look of "Hey, what are you doing in my neighborhood?"

Another time, Evans and I went to Lee's bank so he could withdraw some cash. Lee was buying the eight track stereo system my father had made for me for my twenty-first birthday. Eight track tapes were popular but were mainly for use in a car, but this one was set up in my living room. The reason I could play it in my apartment was because my dad built into the system a AC/DC power converter to power the eight track player. The three-piece system came complete with two nicely covered speakers. I had hardly unwrapped it and got it set up when Evans came over to the apartment to visit. Right away he wanted to know how he could get one for his brother's birthday coming up in a few days. I explained how my dad had made it for my birthday and I had just set it up. But Evans really wanted it. After conversing over the phone with dad, we settled on a price and dad agreed to make me a new one. So it was off to the bank to get the cash.

The trip to the bank gave me the opportunity to observe firsthand experiences blacks have, experiences I had never been aware of before. As we entered the bank, the white guard who had been sitting stood up, as to appear to be extra alert if any problems developed. The tellers started to glance around at each other as if expecting trouble. Even though this was Evans' regular bank and he had adequate funds in his account to cover the amount he was withdrawing, the teller double checked everything and had a short conversation with a man at a desk behind the tellers. In this case, Evans did not have to point out to me the increased tension his presence created. I noticed it and felt it on my own.

There were other times we would be shopping or be out to eat a meal and Lee would point out additional small, but not insignificant, slights he would face. While standing in a store or sitting in a restaurant together, a white clerk or waitress would tend to talk to me and ignore Lee. I cannot say for sure that the person talking to us was ignoring Evans intentionally and this was some overt act of racism. But the scenario was played out consistently. Again, I would not even notice this was going on until he pointed it out. It was true.

Along with all of these issues, growing an Afro created new issues for Evans. Trying to find a barber who could trim his new Afro and not ruin it was a challenge. He eventually found a man on the East side of San Jose. There was a new learning curve for barbers.

I also became aware of prejudicial statements used a lot by me and other whites, "He is really smart for a black guy" or "He is handsome for a black." I was so used to adding the caveat, I didn't notice what I was saying. Another one is "you people," used to accentuate differences between people. After being made aware of this tendency several times, I finally was able to stop using these stereotypical and offensive phrases.

Evans allowed me to challenge and question him on his experiences and personal views of racism. Just like the "Good job, Lee," I felt sometimes he was making something out of nothing. The hardest lessons for me were the implied slights going on around us. The overt and hateful words were easy. But being with him and watching white people's indirect reactions toward him convinced me he was right. Implied forms of racism are just as destructive and hurtful as overt forms.

It is hard for a white person to feel what a black or any minority feels when they know they are being looked down upon or judged. My background was devoid of anything close to what Evans experienced. It was both painful and frustrating to see the truth. I remember wondering why people didn't take the time to get to know him instead of making a decision about him based on the color of his skin. It was all so unfair. As I learned about the history of slavery and the current conditions for blacks in our Southern states, the more I understood in a small way the levels of frustration many blacks were experiencing, frustrations that led some to take drastic actions.

Chapter Nine

A Track Meet to Remember

In 1968, San Jose State hosted the track team from Brigham Young University for a dual meet. In preparing for the meet, we were told something that had happened the year before. In the spring of 1967, San Jose traveled to Utah to compete against BYU, a Mormon University. At this time in the history of the Mormon Church, a certain level of apartheid was being practiced with regards to non-whites. The rumor was non-whites were considered less than qualified to experience the fullness of the Mormon faith. I am not an expert on Mormon history so I can only relate to you what was told to me at the time and what I have learned since then.

In 1967, when the track team arrived on the BYU campus, the San Jose State black track athletes were not allowed to eat or sleep in certain buildings. Those buildings were for the white athletes only. As a result of this whites only policy, the manner in which the black athletes, some greatest trackmen in the world, were treated was hurtful and embarrassing. Evans told me he, Tommie Smith and all the other blacks had to eat in a separate cafeteria and sleep in a special location away from the regular dorms (i.e. white dorms). This was a very unpleasant and humiliating experience. The athletes were very unhappy with this treatment.

In 1968, it was San Jose State's turn to host BYU in San Jose. The athletes that were on the team the year before were still upset about the treatment they received. The story of the bad experience at BYU was related to us at a special team meeting. As a result of the meeting, a commitment was made by the whole team to give some pay back for the poor treatment the black athletes had received in Provo. The payback was not to be done in a hateful manner or with restrictions from certain buildings and cafeterias, but dominance on the track. We were all encouraged to be extra ready for our best performances that day.

As a show of unity and to make a statement against any form of racism and specifically against the bias by the Mormons of that time toward blacks, all of us on the team were designated as honorary blacks for that meet. We wore black armbands to show our solidarity with our black teammates. The whole team was taking a united stand against the shameful treatment our teammates received the year before. A good beating on the track was an appropriate way to respond.

Emotions were charged and everyone had a little extra edge of intensity. It was no longer just a dual meet between two schools, it was now a chance to rally for civil rights and equality. The Civil Rights movement had taken on many different forms during the '60s and many of us felt this was a good, non-violent way to let others know it was time for change. Every victory by a black athlete over a BYU athlete took on special meaning. As a white athlete, I felt proud to represent our black track brothers. It was a privilege to be counted among those that stood against racism.

We all competed at our best and soundly defeated a good BYU team eighty-nine to fifty-six. Carlos, Ronnie Ray Smith and Sam Davis swept the 100-meter dash. Carlos also won the 200-meter dash. Evans won the 400 and Neville Myton and Jack Malloy took first and second in the 800. John Powell won the discus throw and Richard Marks the shot put. Our hurdlers and other field event men held up well also scoring key points.

However, two athletes that stood out above everyone else were Pete Santos and Ralph Gamez. Santos ran an impressive time in the mile, winning his race, and Gamez won the two-mile. Both men doubled that day, Santos coming back in the two-mile and scoring second place points and Gamez getting second in the mile before winning the two-mile.

The day was about showing honor to the black athletes, but two Hispanic runners stole the show. The black athletes showed great appreciation to Santos and Gamez for the extra effort they made to insure victory. The next week we were all made honorary Mexicans as a tribute to Santos and Gamez. The camaraderie on the team was real. Color made no difference, after that we were truly a united group of men with a strong dual purpose—to fight racism and win track meets. In every meet from that day on, I could sense the support of my teammates while running my race. Even with so many great athletes, no one expected to be treated as a star. We were all in this together.

The feelings in the meet with BYU were not about hate and revenge, but about equality and justice. To be fair to the BYU athletes, I never once saw any of them show anything but respect and care for everyone competing in the meet even though they were representing an institution that supported beliefs and doctrines contrary to the basic tenants of the Civil Rights Movement. I never felt the intensity during the meet to mean anything more than a love for fairness and equality among all men. Being hateful was not the point. There was a mutual respect between both teams as athletes who loved to compete at a high level. The men wearing BYU on their jerseys were not the focus, only the school's policies against minorities.

I remember feeling very emotional at times during the meet, sometimes shedding tears of joy as I could see what winning individual races and the overall meet meant to the blacks on the team. There was something very redemptive about the day and I was proud to play a small part in it.

Chapter Ten

Mexico City 1968 Part 1

The Background of the Protest

The 1968 Olympics in Mexico City had many memorable moments. World track records set at these games would last for years into the future. The performances on the track brought the United States to a new level of respect in the world. While performing at the high altitude of 7,000 feet, the U.S. track team showed how well prepared they were for the challenges associated with thin air. But these performances are not the main reason it is remembered.

Many people remember these Olympic for what is called "The Black Power Salute" by Tommie Smith and John Carlos and are still outraged. Smith and Carlos finished first and third in the 200-meters and chose the medal ceremony as a place to make a statement. People today speak with anger about how Smith and Carlos chose to express their views. "Right message, wrong place, wrong time," is what some say about the salute.

The two runners stood on the victory stand with their heads bowed. By wearing black socks and no shoes they represented black poverty and each man raised a black-gloved fist. Smith wore a black scarf around his neck to represent black pride, Carlos had his tracksuit top unzipped to show solidarity with all blue collar workers in the United States and wore a beaded necklace which stood for those individuals who were lynched, hung, tarred or killed that no one said a prayer for. It was for those thrown off the side of the boats in the Middle Passage. (The Middle Passage describes the voyage that brought enslaved Africans across the Atlantic Ocean to North America and the West Indies.)

To many, their actions were very disrespectful and unpatriotic. Both Americans and people from around the world were outraged Smith and Carlos would use the Olympics to make a political statement. To some it felt like they had desecrated a very sacred event.

Within hours of the ceremony, the two Americans were condemned by the International Olympic Committee for their demonstration on the victory stand. A spokesperson for the organization said it was "a deliberate and violent breach of the fundamental principles of the Olympic spirit."

I have a different point of view about the protest. Being a teammate with these men I knew the real issues behind the protest. It is important to understand the events that led up to Mexico City. Smith and Carlos were courageous patriots wanting to express their sorrow about how not everyone living in the United States had the opportunity to experience all this great country has to offer. They wanted to highlight the plight of African American men and women in the United States. It is now time to view their actions in a positive light.

Through education and life experiences, Smith and Carlos came to understand they had a responsibility and duty to use their moment as the world watched to point out the problems blacks in the U.S. were facing. Even though the Civil Rights Act had been passed in 1964 and schools had been ordered to desegregate in the mid-1950s, society had a long way to go as far as bringing "Liberty and Justice for all" to minorities, especially blacks in our southern states. Smith and Carlos' hearts were for the thousands and thousands of blacks living under the cloud of racism and racial inequality. I believe they had no desire to promote the "Black Power" movement that was associated with violence. They simply wanted to draw world attention to the depth of the unique problems blacks were facing.

Some did see it as an extension of the "Black Power" movement, connecting their demonstration with a radical and sometimes violent element of protesters making the news in cities across America. From what I observed any connection with violence could not have been further from the truth. Understanding the issues leading up to the Olympics gave me a clearer perspective on the protest. What were those issues?

A big issue for the athletes was Avery Brundage, head of the International Olympic committee. In today's global political climate, no one thinks twice about denouncing anyone who even appears to be supportive of Adolph Hitler and the Third Reich. The mere mention in a slightly positive manner of the man and his reign of terror can get a lot of negative press. I remember when in May of 1996, Marge Schott, the former owner of Major League baseball's Cincinnati Reds mentioned Hitler was good when he came into power but he went too far. She was banned by major League Baseball.

The fight over apartheid has changed the landscape of South Africa. Anyone supporting the old system would be shouted down in any public forum today.

A person adhering to the belief black Americans are inferior in intelligence would not be considered for any prominent office or position of leadership. And if any person believed blacks should just be grateful for being able to participate in sports and should keep quiet about any social or economic disparities African Americans are facing, would be met with even harsher criticism.

So, if anyone holding any of these views, let alone all three, attempted to lead a major international event today, like the

Olympics, he or she would be censured. Protests would abound and most likely the event would not move forward until he or she was removed. Not so back in the 1960s. There is evidence suggesting Avery Brundage, the head of the International Olympic Committee, was one who may have harbored all of these beliefs and prejudices. The following quotes testify to some of his feelings, quotes that set him as an adversary to the black athlete.

"It seems a little ungrateful to attempt to boycott something which has given them such great opportunity," said Brundage when faced with the possibility of a walkout by the Negro athlete in the summer of 1968. "Sure there's a racial problem. But of all Negroes, reason many whites, the athlete has the least to complain about. Why can't he be a credit to his race like Jesse Owens?"[12]

These quotes created an animosity between Brundage and the black athletes. They also created a bad image for the black athlete. *Newsweek* ran a cover story in July of 1968 featuring a running Tommie Smith with the headline "The Angry Black Athlete." This article did not help these men or their cause. Although many Americans were angry about the treatment our black citizens were getting, *Newsweek* seemed to single them out as extra angry and anti-American. I wonder what the reaction toward them would have been had the headline read "The Socially Conscious Black Athlete."

The truth was Owens' life was not so great after the Olympics. Great black athletes like Jackie Robinson, Bill Russell and Muhammad Ali were supportive of a potential boycott. Lew Alcindor (Kareem Abdul-Jabbar) boycotted the Olympic trials.

The *Newsweek* article painted a picture of rebellion and dis-organization. It did provide some evidence as to why some black athletes were indeed angry and for good reason. One athlete

---

12 Axthelm, Pete, "The Angry Black Athlete," *Newsweek*, July 15, 1968, 57.

quit the Stanford track team when he overheard the head coach, Payton Jordan, talking about "a N-word in the woodpile." Jordon was USA's head track coach for the '68 Olympic team.[13]

This labeling of black athletes as "angry" or "militant," as opposed to socially conscious and compassionate for the underdog, put the athletes in an odd position. The article said it became obvious "they were going to use their talent on the field toward an ideological end: nothing less than an attack on racial injustice in American life," as if that was a bad thing.[14]

The message of Harry Edwards, a sociology professor at San Jose State was resonating with many athletes who were aware of the many social injustices most black Americans were facing. "Athletes are on the field maybe four hours a day. The rest of the time, they're in the same garbage heap that most of the black people in this society live in... Black Athletes must take a stand."[15] All blacks, athletes and non-athletes alike, were feeling the frustration of the lack of progress in bringing equality to African Americans.

What were some of the factors that led to this frustration? Much of the lack of progress in civil rights fell in the laps of our Presidents. Michael Klarman gave a clear historical run-down of the slowness of our Presidents when dealing with Civil Rights in a recent article. Klarman is a professor at Harvard Law School and the author of *From Jim Crow to Civil Rights*, which won the 2005 Bancroft Prize.

His explanation helps me to see what rights activates have been up against for years.

"It is difficult to ask historically disadvantaged minority groups to be patient in waiting for full recognition of their

---

13 Axthelm, Pete, "The Angry Black Athlete, *Newsweek*, July 15, 1968, 57.

14 Axthelm, Pete, "The Angry Black Athlete, *Newsweek*, July 15, 1968, 56.

15 Axthelm, Pete, "The Angry Black Athlete, *Newsweek*, July 15, 1968, 57.

constitutional rights. Thurgood Marshall, the great NAACP organizer and litigator, was asked after Brown vs. Board of Education whether, in light of threatened violence and school closures in the South (in the 1950s), he would have been 'well advised to let things move along gradually for a while.' Marshall responded that he did indeed believe in gradualism, but 'I also believe that 90-odd-years [the time elapsed since the Emancipation Proclamation] is pretty gradual.'

"Historically, American presidents have rarely gotten far ahead of public opinion on civil rights issues, and the few times they have, they've paid a substantial price for doing so.[16]

Following is a summary of the article, which can be read in full in appendix 4.

"President Lincoln, known to history as the Great Emancipator, was a relative latecomer to the abolitionist cause. It was, in the end, battlefield losses during the Civil War that forced him, almost as an act of desperation, to free slaves in order to undermine the Confederate labor supply and strengthen Union military forces. African American voters ended their decades-long loyalty to the Republican Party in the 1930s because President Franklin D. Roosevelt generally included blacks in the assistance offered by his New Deal. But even then, Roosevelt steadfastly refused to support federal anti-lynching and anti-poll tax legislation during his more than three terms in office. Why? Because the white South remained a vital component of the political coalition that had elected him. In 1948, President Truman issued landmark executive orders desegregating the federal military and civil service. But he did so only after advisers warned him, following the disastrous 1946 off-year congressional elections, that his only chance of reelection was taking a disproportionate share of the African American vote in the North. During the first two years of his presidency, John F. Kennedy refused to support civil rights legislation, which would have alienated the Southern Democrats who had proved vital

to his election in 1960 and whom he was likely to need again in 1964.[17]

Black athletes speaking out about these social and racial issues in the 1960s were not well received. Instead of being viewed as heroic political activists with a strong love for their country, these men's lives were threatened for even hinting at a boycott of the Olympics. Instead of being hailed as culturally aware and caring young men, they were vilified. But, they had the courage to stand up for what was wrong.

These quotes from Smith and Carlos in 2008 sum it up:

"I went up there as a dignified black man and said: 'What's going on is wrong,'" Carlos says.

Their protest, Smith says, *"was a cry for freedom and for human rights. We had to be seen because we couldn't be heard."*[18]

For me, it is helpful to understand how all of these issues formed the emotionally charged backdrop in the months leading up to the 1968 Olympics in Mexico City. Many of these issues centered around Brundage and his views on black athletes, Jews and South Africans. The biggest issue influencing the athletes was the long history in the United States of abusive treatment of blacks combined with the lack of meaningful progress toward creating a society of equality. The motivation to make a statement was strong. Hearts were aching for those who were being mistreated under our flag. How is the "salute" viewed now?

---

16 Michael Klarman, "The civil rights trap." *L.A. Times*, September 19, 2010, A 36.

17 Michael Klarman, "The civil rights trap." *L.A. Times*, September 19, 2010, A 36.

18 Davis, David, "Olympic Athletes Who took a Stand," *Smithsonian.com*, August 2008, http://www.smithsonianmag.com/people-places/indelible-olympics-200808. html#ixzz0ogGbq2sm

Chapter Eleven

Mexico City Part 2

In 2008 on ESPN, Smith and Carlos were awarded an ESPY called the Arthur Ashe Courage Award. In an excellent short video narrated by Tom Cruise, the events surrounding the Mexico City "Black Power" salute were presented. Cruise talked about the way Smith and Carlos approached the medal stand, explaining how they carried their shoes to symbolize the poverty of their youth. Smith went on to describe his upraised fist as "a prayer."

"My prayer was for solidarity. A prayer of hope, hope that we could unite as a people instead of being separatists in a country that is supposed to be one."

A protest AND a prayer. Smith and Carlos meant it for good, and had staked their careers on the message it would send. Though they were booed as they left the medal stand, the poster of that protest is one of the most enduring images of the Civil Rights Movement, and perhaps the most energizing.

There are many strong opposing views about what these men did in their symbolic protest. Within a week of the ESPY broadcast, Jonah Goldberg of the Jewish World Review wrote an article panning ESPN for honoring the men and their "salute." He, like many, connected the "salute" with the Black Panthers and called it an obscene gesture. He goes as far as tying the slaughter of the Israeli athletes by Palestinian terrorists the 1972

Olympics to the "salute." This Op-Ed was subsequently printed in the L.A. Times drawing lots of reaction from both sides.[19]

I wonder if, in 1968, more people had KNOWN the true historical, sociological and cultural meaning of the protest, there may have been a broader base of support from both blacks and whites? The truth is not even all blacks supported Smith and Carlos, but those that did, did so with enthusiasm. Black supporters felt empowered, vindicated, victorious, and beautiful, for the first time.

Knowing them personally and competing on the track with them gave me a different perspective about the demonstration. My perspective at the time was not a popular one. Even to this day, for some people, it is very unpopular and tends to raise levels of strong emotion in those who disagree. Never the less, I tried to understand what they were saying by putting it into the context of the cultural changes that were taking place along with their hearts as compassionate and caring men.

I do not claim to know everything about this. In fact, I know very little in comparison to Evans, Smith, and Carlos. I want to be very careful not to misrepresent them or their motives. I was not in Mexico City and can only relate what I heard at the time from those who were there and subsequent conversations with Evans, Smith, and Carlos. This is certainly not an official version or one even endorsed by Carlos and Smith. It is only my perspective.

As I said in the last chapter, it was through education and life experiences that Smith, Carlos and Evans came to understand they had a responsibility and duty to use their success in athletics to point out the plight of blacks in the U.S. Even though the Civil Rights Act had been passed in 1964, society had a long way to go as far as bringing "Liberty and Justice for all" to all minorities,

---

19 Jonah Goldberg, "68 Olympic salute deserves no honor," *Jewish World Review* July 30, 2008, 27.

especially blacks and especially in our Southern states.

In 1954, the Supreme Court ruled that separate but equal schools were unconstitutional. The federal government's actions to enforce this rule in Little Rock, Arkansas in 1957 started an ugly and violent chapter in our history. Arkansas Gov. Orval Faubus sent National Guard troops to block nine African American students from entering Central High School. President Dwight Eisenhower countered with the Army's 101st Airborne Division to surround the students and walk them into the school.[20]

As the civil rights movement took root in the Southern states, there are many stories of lynchings and fire bombings during the fifties and sixties Many of the crimes against blacks were never investigated or the cases were dismissed. The treatment of blacks was horrible from all accounts in our history books. The struggle for equality was violent as whites and members of the Ku Klux Klan fought for the status quo. People were dying throughout the country. All of this was not lost on Evans, Smith and Carlos.

Their hearts were for the "brothers and sisters" living under the cloud of racism and racial inequality. As far as I knew, they had no desire to promote the "Black Power" movement that was associated with violence. They simply wanted to draw world attention to the depth of the unique problems blacks were facing.

After the demonstration, Smith and Carlos were forced to leave the Olympic village. The criticisms came fast and hard. The peaceful, non-violent demonstration demonized Smith and Carlos to the American public. They returned to San Jose as personae non-grata. Life was not easy. To some, they became villains and anti-American. It was sad to watch. Even to this day, my experience has been that even a mention of the "Salute" to

---

20 Keith Thursby, "One of the Little Rock Nine." Los Angeles Times, September 7, 2010, AA.

non-blacks of my generation brings a strong negative reaction. My attempts to explain the truth, brings even more negative reaction.

Today, the "salute" by Smith and Carlos is viewed in a favorable manner by a growing number of people. There is a larger than life statue of the "salute" on the San Jose State campus honoring them. My most recent contact with Smith was in 2008, his last year of coaching track at Santa Monica College and just before he moved to Georgia. He autographed my poster of the "Salute."

During our conversation, he reminded me the demonstration was well thought out ahead of time and not a last minute, thrown together action. I mentioned a rumor I heard that the protest was a spur of the moment decision. Tommie is a very intelligent man and takes offense at any suggestion that this was a spur of the moment idea.

The reason I mentioned some thought about the protest being a spur of the moment decision to Smith was because I heard a version of the story from Neville Myton, a Jamaican 400-meter runner and Olympian. Myton and I shared an apartment at San Jose State along with two other athletes. After the Olympics, Myton told me his version of what he saw while sitting in the stands with Smith, Carlos and their families. He felt that the salute was a last minute decision and the men really didn't have a plan until just before the medal presentation. The truth is there was a change in the plan and Myton saw it, but, according to Smith, it was still well thought out.

What changed? The initial focus of the protest was to be against Brundage, the president of the IOC. As was pointed out earlier, he was considered by some to be a racist, an Anti-Semite and pro-Nazi. Before the 1968 Games, there were reports that Evans, Smith and Carlos were considering a boycott of the games. A lot of things were said about them, some true, but most false. At the Olympic trials in Los Angeles in the summer of '68 there was an attempt to get consensus among the athletes to organize a boycott. The idea of a boycott failed.

During the year before the Olympics, Evans, Smith and others did start a movement called the Olympic Project for Human Rights ("OPHR"). Starting this organization only increased the angst among the leadership of both the United States Olympic Committee and the International Olympic Committee. The aim of the organization was to protest racial segregation in the United States and elsewhere (such as South Africa). Smith has noted that the project was about human rights, of "all humanity, even those who denied us ours," according to his autobiography *Silent Gesture—Autobiography of Tommie Smith*. Eventually, in lieu of a boycott, it was left up to each athlete to protest in any way he felt comfortable with.

Brundage reacted strongly against the OPHR and talk of a boycott and protests. He made reckless comments toward the OPHR movement when he called the leaders "misguided young men" and "a little ungrateful." This only strengthened the resolve of the athletes to make their position heard. This combined with his history of not condemning the pro-Nazi Hitler salute in the 1936 Olympics, his attempts to include white South African athletes in the Olympics and his stance against athletic contests being held hostage to cries of human rights violations, made him an appropriate target for protest.

Thinking Brundage would hand them their medals and shake their hands, the plan was to wear gloves to avoid touching his bare hand. This would send the world a message of discontent and reveal his positions on race and human rights. As a silent protest they would avoid touching his skin. The plan was modified when they realized he would not be handing out the medals. They now needed a new form of protest.

The reason for Myton's confusion was because Carlos had

left his black gloves in the village, so the two men only had one pair between them. What Myton saw was not a hurried last minute creation of a protest, but an adjustment made to compensate for them only having one pair of gloves. To Myton, it appeared they were spontaneously planning what to do just minutes before the ceremony. Carlos says much of it was a last minute adjustment and happened much like Myton had described. This caused a rift between Smith and Carlos. Adding to the rift is Carlos' statement about letting Smith win the 200 so Smith could set the pace for the protest.

A July 2008 article in the *L.A. Times* revealed Smith and Carlos are at odds as to who planned the protest and how the race unfolded. The schism is over things Smith said about the protest and Carlos' role in his book *Silent Gesture*. In a phone conversation, Carlos said to me "Smith's book is trash." He also says that he "let up" to allow Smith to win the 200-meter race. Smith disagrees. Both men claim responsibility for planning the protest. Smith claims he told Carlos just to follow his example and do what he did if he wanted to. Carlos says he is the one who told Smith that they needed to make some sort of statement. I have a personal opinion about what I think happened, but I like what Evans says in his book after describing the disagreement. *"Leave it, either way, and record what happened."*[21] I hope the importance of what they did will not be lost in the controversy over whose idea it was and who the leader was.

Harry Edwards sums it all up with this quote: *"What matters is their courageousness. One hundred years from now, what will matter was that their gesture became the iconic image of a phenomenal era, when people from Muhammad Ali to Curt Flood changed the face, the image and the dynamics of American sport."*[22]

---

21 Murphy, The Last Protest: Lee Evans in Mexico City, 263.

22 David Davis, "Once United, Now Divided." Los Angeles Times, July 8, 2008, 1.

Chapter Twelve

"Then I won't run."

Evans threatened.

After Smith and Carlos did the "Salute," Brundage forced them to leave the Olympic Village within twenty-four hours with the threat that the entire American track and field team would not be allowed to compete in the remaining two days of events. President Brundage was angry with Smith and Carlos, but he was not done. He threatened Evans, before he even ran.

Evans told me what Brundage said to him. I am not sure how widely spread this story is, but he told it to me in a conversation at his apartment as we looked at his two gold medals.

Brundage came to Evans and said he knew he was going to win the 400-meters and set both Olympic and world records. Brundage so feared Evans was going to do something similar to what Smith and Carlos had done, he told him if he so much as twitched on the victory stand, he would be putting the whole American team at risk of being expelled. He made it very clear if Evans had any plans to do something, there would be big trouble.

Any plans Evans had to protest ended. He was in support of what had already been done, but he did not see himself furthering the protest. Additional protests would only distract from what his teammates had done, not add to it.

But the threat shook him up. He did not want to carry the weight of that responsibility on his shoulders. He reasoned that something odd could happen. He could sneeze, or a bee could land on him, anything that would cause him to react. He knew that his actions would be interpreted as another form of protest, causing pain to all the athletes from the U.S.

Feeling that pressure, he decided to skip the race and leave himself. This was not an easy decision but one he felt was correct. He packed his bags and headed out of the village. Fortunately, Bud Winter, our San Jose coach, caught up with him as he was getting on the elevator in the village dorms. Evans, being a caring and sensitive man, was torn up inside over everything that was happening.

The elevator scene Evans described was emotional and intense. Evans was very upset about the threat. He was being hounded by the media wherever he went in the village. Through eyes filled with tears, he explained to coach how he was angry with Brundage for threatening him. The thought he could be responsible for ruining the Olympics for the rest of the American team ate away at him. He also knew leaving would most likely take away his only chance to win Olympic gold. Not doing so would be a great disappointment. After a long and at times contentious discussion in the elevator, Evans relented on his choice to leave. Coach Winter's message was plain and straight-forward as he helped Evans see this was his time to run. "Opportunities to win an Olympic Gold medal while setting Olympic and World records don't come but usually once in a lifetime and you shouldn't let it pass," coach Winter emphasized.

Smith and Carlos both encouraged him to run also. They told him to run and to win. With their encouragement along with coach Winter's, he moved forward. And run he did, setting a record that lasted until 1988. His time of 43.86 was phenomenal. He did wear a black beret on the medal stand as a mild form of protest, but it was so minor compared to what had already happened, no one said anything.

Evans went on to also anchor the 4 x 400 relay team for another gold medal. After the '68 Games, Evans was in an awkward situation. He was largely ignored by the white community because he was considered to be a militant. Even with all this success there were no parades for him when he returned. He was subject to criticism, not as severe as Smith and Carlos were receiving, but still painful. What made it even more difficult was many of his detractors were African Americans.

Some blacks felt he should have visibly protested and been less friendly on the victory stand. He wore a beret, waved to the crowd and smiled. His post race comments got him in further trouble with his black peers when he acknowledged that he "owed a debt of gratitude to his white coach Bud Winter" and that "he dedicated his victories at the Olympics not only to all black people but also his many 'white friends.'" I am happy to be counted among those "white friends."

These records and medals did not change him. Competing in college dual meets was not a come down after all of the glory of the Olympics. His resolve to lead San Jose State to a national championship was as strong as ever. By June of 1969, he reached that goal. With fellow Olympians Ronnie Ray Smith, Carlos, Greek pole-vaulter Chris Papanicolaou and several other future Olympians including discus thrower John Powell, four-time American Olympian, San Jose State scored a major victory. I did not run a qualifying time to compete in the meet and was not on the trip to Knoxville, Tennessee, but Evans sent me a postcard wishing I were there with him and the team. I still have the postcard.

As an individual, Evans attained great success, but I really believe he got more joy out of seeing the team succeed. I think he also got satisfaction out of seeing his teammates gain personal success in their individual events, cheering everyone on during track meets.

All Photos by Jeff Kroot unless noted.

SPEED CITY: SAN JOSE, CA - MARCH 1968
(Photo by Jeff Kroot)
Top L-R: Kirk Clayton (9.3), Jerry Williams (9.4), Sam Davis (9.4),
Bill Gaines (9.3), Lee Evans (20.7, 45.2), Bob Griffin (9.5), Frank Slaton (9.5)
Bottom L-R: Tommie Smith (9.3, 20.0, 44.8), Ronnie Ray Smith (9.4, 20.9), John Carlos (9.4, 20.3)

The men of Speed City

Smith runs World Record 44.5 on old San Jose track, May 1967. Evans 2nd.

Carlos wins 100, 1968
L to R, Kirk Clayton, Ronnie Ray Smith, Sam Davis

Carlos wins 100, 1969

Carlos and Evans 1969

Carlos and Smith stretch, 1968

Evans runs a leg in the 1600-meter relay in International Games in the Los Angles Coliseum. A World Record and the first team to run under 3:00 at 2:59.6

Evans anchors 1600 meter Relay In Commonwealth Games,
1967 Beating Domansky at the Los Angeles Coliseum.

Adkins, Evans and Bud Winter, 1969
(Photo by Dave Funderburk)

Adkins wins mile in 4:09.2 against
Washington at San Jose, 1969
(Photo by Dave Funderburk)

Chapter Thirteen

"The True Lee"

After the Olympics in the fall of 1968, there was another incident involving San Jose State and BYU, but this time on the football field. Seven black players on the San Jose team refused to suit up and play against BYU as a protest toward the Mormons' attitudes toward blacks. This caused a stir on campus, especially when the President of San Jose State made plans to take away these athletes' scholarships.

During the fall of 1968, our track team had regular Friday night meetings, gearing up for the start of what would become a championship season. We would gather in a large classroom in the athletic department building and talk about team unity, work outs etc. These Friday night "pep rally meetings" were attended by the coaches and trainers also.

The San Jose State President's threat toward the football players created an increased sensitivity about race relations. The arguments were bouncing between responsibility and racism. To not support the actions of the players was paramount to agreeing with the doctrines of the Mormon Church. To agree with the President was siding with unfairness and insensitivity to the issues of racism. Tension was on the rise. Threats and counter threats were being thrown around. This was a micro example of the tension and unrest seen on a national scale during the Civil Rights Movement. All of this was intensified because of the "Salute" in Mexico City.

At one of our regular Friday night meetings, an outsider attended. John Carlos invited James Edwards, younger brother of Harry Edwards, (the San Jose State sociology professor and a major supporter of the boycott of the Olympics by the black athletes), to the meeting. He had come from Fresno to make a request of the white athletes on the team. He was asking the white athletes to give up our scholarships in protest of the President's actions against the football players.

We were all curious about this request. James Edwards was not a student at San Jose State and was not a familiar face to all of us on the team. We had lots of questions about the effectiveness of the move. Emotions quickly rose as the discussion progressed. Basically Carlos and Edwards led the meeting and strongly suggested we take action and take it now! Attempts to ask questions like "Help us understand the issues and how this will help?" were met with retorts of "Where have you been all your life? Get your head out of the sand. How can you not understand the issues?" In a certain way I felt intimidated and frustrated. This was not Carlos and Edward's intention, it just came across in a way I was not used to. I know now their hearts were right and I am only reflecting how it felt at the time.

I, along with most on the team, was on the side of the football players and against the treatment they were receiving, but I was not sure giving up my scholarship was the best way to help them. I expressed to Carlos the fact my scholarship did not cover all my costs and my parents were making up the difference. Imagining how they would respond created increased tension inside of me. Mentioning this angle led to further retorts by Carlos and Edwards about the need to stand for these players.

The white athletes asked for time to think about it. The request for time was met with retorts of "Time? What is there to think about?" Carlos and Edwards agreed to give us some time to think about it, agreeing to let us sleep on it. We planned to meet again on Saturday morning and make a decision about what to do. The cooling off period proved to be very valuable.

Truly I did not know what to do so I turned to Evans for advice. I told him I wanted to do what was right, but I really did not know what the best course of action was. He knew my heart was right, but he could see the confusion; not only mine, but everyone's. At this point, Lee rose to the challenge and showed what a true friend he was.

Evans pulled me aside along with another white athlete, Bob Slover, and we talked about the rumors we had heard about Harry Edwards making lots of money speaking at East Coast Universities. He had become a popular speaker giving speeches about his experiences with Smith and Carlos. There was a feeling he had climbed the backs of the black athletes and made a profit for himself speaking at East Coast Universities. At the same time, we heard Smith and Carlos were having a hard time financially in their post "salute" lives. Was it possible our visitor—James Edwards—was more interested in making a name for himself than he was in the plight of the football players? Did Harry Edwards know what his brother James was doing? At best, we wondered if there were mixed motives in his plan. Was there more behind the scenes?

Evans calmly talked these issues over with Sloan and me. With Evans' help, we concluded we needed to do something to show support other than giving up our scholarships. Evans agreed if we felt James Edwards was doing this to enhance his image and make money we should not submit to his leadership. If following Edward's plan would do more for him than the football players, we should come up with a better plan and ignore his. Slover and I realized this was not a decision for the two of us, but one all the white members needed to discuss. We asked Lee if he would join us and meet with the white team members to help us develop a new plan. He agreed. We hastily organized an impromptu meeting at the house of another teammate later in the evening.

In being willing to talk to all the white athletes, Evans showed great courage and a real strength of character. There was a certain level of risk involved in this move, but friendship was what was most important to Evans. I walked with Evans to the meeting that night. We zigzagged through the streets in the neighborhood adjacent to the college, always checking over our shoulders to make sure we were not being followed. It was very important for Evans to keep this a confidential meeting. Being seen as a traitor would not have been good for him, even though what he was doing was not subversive to the cause of the black athlete. But there was a big chance his actions would be misunderstood. I was proud to walk with him that night. It gave me a chance to get a glimpse of the pressure he was under after the Olympics. He was being pulled in many directions and was rethinking many issues in his life.

Once at the house, with drapes drawn, Evans listened to our concerns about this not being an issue of race when it came to Edwards' involvement. We explained our suspicions about being used for the purpose of promoting a person, not a cause.

Without making a judgment about James Edwards' motives, Evans helped us discuss a strategy that would help the football players by sending a message to the San Jose State President. Our plan put to ease our concerns about promoting a person and without causing financial damage to anyone. I think Evans drew on something Smith had said a year earlier.

In an interview by Dick Drake of *Track and Field News* in 1967, Smith and Evans were asked about a possible boycott of the '68 Olympics. Drake asked them, "Why boycott only the Olympics? Why single them out for boycotting, while continuing to compete for a school which has been charged with discrimination and in a country where it exists?" I think Tommie Smith's answer about education and scholarships influenced Evans' thinking and was a factor in his discussion with the white athletes.

"Why should we boycott the Olympics instead of the meets at our college? A good percentage of the Negroes are in college because of a scholarship. Now, if we discontinue athletics, the scholarship almost means our lives to us. I got my education through a scholarship. If I had discontinued competition, it would have meant that my scholarship would have been taken away. Therefore, I wouldn't have gotten an education and gotten as far as I have, and so I wouldn't know what I'm talking about. Education is a prelude to a later advancement in life: knowledge. Therefore, unless you have the financial background, discontinuing athletics wouldn't be advantageous to any cause. "[23] The full interview can be read in appendix 1.

Lee was not against Carlos and Edwards. He agreed with everyone's desire to send a strong message to the President to point out his actions were unacceptable. Something had to be done. Evans also understood Smith's point made a year earlier and was broadening it to include white and Hispanic athletes also. I was proud of my friend for his courage to step up and help us with our confusion at the risk of being misunderstood and ostracized by fellow blacks.

The issue was resolved before we met the next day to reveal our new plan. The President issued a statement saying he was not going to take away the scholarships. Instead, the players were absolved and allowed to continue playing the rest of the season. Carlos says today he thinks there was even more going on behind the scenes. He told me in 2010 about two new "students" who seemingly appeared out of nowhere on campus during this controversy and befriended him. He doesn't know for sure, but he believes they were government agents, possibly from the FBI. Why they were on campus and what they accomplished is a mystery to this day. According to John, they were gone as quickly as they appeared. To me, it makes sense the federal government would be concerned about the scholarship issue

---

23 Dick Drake, "In Their Own Words," November, 1967.

turning into a major event, a civil disturbance, so they wanted to monitor activities surrounding this controversy.

The white athletes were ready to stand with the football players and voice our unhappiness with the situation. We were not the group of insensitive white guys we may have appeared to be the night of the meeting. We just wanted to make sure we were doing the right thing. Sometimes a good decision can only be made with solid discussion, not while being pressured.

The BYU track meet and the football players' protest against BYU was another step of growth in my understanding of the painful experiences minorities face in our culture. The Mormons have adjusted their theology since that time, but the reality of life in some parts of the United States, as harsh as it was, opened all of our eyes to the fact that not all was well and far from equal between the races in our country.

I graduated in 1969 and returned to my hometown of Escondido, California. I had strong feelings about my experiences with Evans and the others but was unsure about what difference these experiences would make in my life. It did not take long before I was facing my first "personal fallout" from speaking about the lessons I learned in Speed City.

Chapter Fourteen

"Personal fallout"

After graduating from San Jose State in 1969, I returned to my hometown to work with a church youth program. A friend of mine was a sports reporter for the local newspaper and former high school track teammate. He asked if he could interview me about my experiences at San Jose State. I willingly agreed. The article was mostly about my running successes and my friendship with Evans, but he did ask me about Smith and Carlos' medal stand demonstration.

In my response, I did not condemn Smith and Carlos or express disgust about their actions in Mexico City. I delved into the deeper issue surrounding the controversy. I supported Smith and Carlos, saying their demonstration was necessary and needed to be made. I said the "salute" was meant to draw attention to our nation's race-relations problems. I also discussed how some felt Smith and Carlos should not have introduced politics to the Olympics. But the truth was, national politics was already very prevalent. Since then, it has played even a bigger role with boycotts by whole blocks of nations.

This is the quote that was in the *Escondido Times-Advocate* on July 4, 1969 in my response to reporter Dave Hoff's question, "Did you agree with the black glove protest of Smith and Carlos at the Olympics?" *"They had to get attention from the world and that was the best place to do it. I think that the President of our school put it pretty well when he said that he couldn't understand how the nation could charge Tommie and John with disrespect when the U.S. is the only country in the world that will not dip its flag in respect to the host nation during the opening ceremonies.* "[24]

In the same article, when asked about the unrest among black athletes, I said: *"They're looking for their identity and their history. White people took that away* (since then I have come to understand that it was not just white people who participated in slave trading). *Ever since the slave days, black people have been told they're stupid and many of them still believe it. Lee Evans told me that he still believed it up until just a couple of years ago. They just want to do something for their people."* [25]

The repercussions of these quotes surprised me. My father, a popular dentist and respected community leader asked me why I said what I said.

"Because I think it is the truth," I said confidently.

"I wish you would not have said it," was his response. "I am disappointed in you for what you said. Do you really believe it?"

"Yes, I do. I know these men and I know why they did what they did. Somebody needs to stand up for what is wrong with the way people are being treated."

"I am getting flak from my country club buddies over the article. They are asking me if my son is a communist, a N-word lover?" He said again he wished I had never said it.

He was hurt and embarrassed. I was shocked. The last thing I wanted to do was hurt my father or cause him embarrassment, but I did. I wish now I would have argued with him. I did not debate with him nor did I apologize. I was disappointed that he put his reputation with his country club buddies ahead of

---

24 Hoff, Dave, "Times are a-changin.'" *Daily Times-Advocate*, July 4, 1969.

25 Ibid.

his relationship with me. In reality, the little bit of harassment he received was minor compared to the suffering thousands of blacks and other minorities have endured over the years.

Besides my father being upset, some of my friends said I was "being used" by the newspaper reporter to push his agenda. I did not see how that could be true. He did not misquote me and he did not sensationalize what I said, he just reported it. I am not sure how he felt about the protest, whether he agreed or disagreed. I think those who said I was "being used" were afraid to express to me how they really felt and were avoiding telling me directly they did not like what I said.

These reactions by my father and friends gave me a clue about the environment in which I was raised. As a young person, I never really gave racism much thought, other than the one contact I had with the man cleaning bricks next door. I never envisioned my hometown as being a place not accepting of any minority choosing to live there.

By now I was beginning to realize how the subtle and not so subtle comments made in my home and around town about minorities did affect me. Jokes would be told that demeaned minorities, but it seemed "normal" to make fun of those that were different. Even a children's counting game about choosing that I played with other children had racial overtones.

Eeny, meeny, miny, moe,

Catch a tiger/monkey/baby by the toe.

If he hollers let him go,

Eeny, meeny, miny, moe.

Adults in my childhood substituted the "N-word" for tiger/ monkey/baby in this rhyme. It was done with no apologies. Negative attitudes toward blacks became even more evident when riots were reported on television during the turbulent Civil Rights Movement in the early '60s.

Another idea that was prevalent during my youth was if a black family moved into a neighborhood, within a short time the whole neighborhood would be black and the property values would drop. I remember hearing about efforts being made to keep the first family from moving in. A popular phrase from that era was "There goes the neighborhood" when a black family moved in.

In retrospect, I can see now that Dr. Martin Luther King, Freedom Marches, forced integration of schools and the lunch counter "sit-ins" in the South were being judged in a negative manner by the adults in my life. I never heard any encouragement toward the "Freedom Marchers" or Rosa Parks and her defiance to Jim Crow laws. Images of blacks being sprayed with fire hoses and attacked by dogs on the TV news shows were met with tacit approval. The influences were subtle, not overt.

Sadly, I can see why my views on the "Salute" were way out of sync with many in my hometown, especially my father's friends. So where did I go from there? I had valuable life experiences from my two years in San Jose, but now I was back in my hometown. I could see I needed to think through what these experiences meant for my future.

After marrying in 1972, I told my wife, Marleen the stories of my glory days in track and about my friendships with these Olympic athletes. I think she sort of believed me, but it sounded pretty far out. I had no contact with Lee Evans for a number of years, we had lost track of each other. But in 1984, my family and I were traveling back to Southern California after spending a week in the Eureka area of Northern California. The six of us had stopped for breakfast at a Denny's in a very desolate spot in central California along the I-5. Marleen and I were sitting at a table with our children, a daughter and three sons ages one to nine, when I heard a voice I recognized. It sounded like Lee Evans. Sure enough it was.

Evans was sitting at the counter with another man having breakfast. I pointed him out and my wife said if my stories were true, now was the time to prove it. I called out his name. He looked over, saw me and said, "Paddle Foot, How are you?" Learning my lesson from the past, I did not respond with "O.K. Crown Head," not knowing who was eating with him. We were excited to see each other after many years. It seemed like no time had passed. He was on his way to Los Angles to attend the 1984 Olympic games, not as an athlete but as a representative for a company he was working for, selling an energy product used by athletes.

It was a great reunion. We caught up on old times and current events. Finally, Marleen believed my stories. My next contact with him wasn't until 2005 after Hurricane Katrina. I had heard he was living in the south and coaching at the University of South Alabama. I had two motivations for contacting him. One was to find out if he was okay and if he needed any help and the second was to offer him the DVD from the 1969 Stanford meet. He was okay following the hurricane and was really happy to get the DVD. He told me while he was in Africa in a previous year, all of his old films and pictures from his running days had been stolen and he had nothing to show his family from his running days. I was glad to send it to him.

He is not coaching in Alabama anymore but is working with the Nigerian Olympic Track and Field Team preparing for the 2012 Olympics in London. He took this position after doing a short stint with the United Nations doing relief work in another part of Africa. He is someone I will always admire and will always be thankful to for the life lessons he taught me.

Chapter Fifteen

"Epilog"

So what impact did all these experiences have on my life? That is not easy to answer. I didn't become a civil rights activist or an attorney fighting for equal rights legislation or even a politician to fight the battle for equality at the state or federal level. I hopefully have lived my life with a deeper understanding of the injustices blacks and other minorities face. I have sought to fight the ugliness of racism whenever confronted with it and to teach equality wherever possible.

Early on, I had an experience that gave me the opportunity to put into practice what I had learned. In October of 1970, I had taken a bus with nearly one hundred eighth graders to a "Haunted House" south of where we lived. It was a fundraiser event for a local youth organization and very popular. I parked the bus and lined the students up in a dark dusty parking lot near the haunted house. I went to the front gate to meet the organizer and get the pre-purchased tickets that would allow us to get into the house faster.

As I returned to the students, I noticed in the headlights of cars further away that something was happening at the back of the line. It appeared that there was a lot of shoving accompanied with screams and shouting. As I got closer, I saw that a group of eight young men were coming up toward the haunted house next to the line of my students. I was close enough now to see there was more than playful shoving going on. The small group of teens were swinging something and hitting the students. I soon discovered they were swinging socks filled with chains and other heavy objects, hitting my students in their faces, arms and backs. They were hurting the students, knocking teeth loose and causing heads to bleed.

Being the leader, I naturally ran up to the attackers and attempted to draw them away from the students and take the hits myself if needed. I really didn't think they would hit an adult. But I was wrong. I now saw it was a group of black youths doing the damage. It seemed maybe they had come on their own or had accidentally found the event and were wandering aimlessly through the parking lot. I found out later the attackers had been brought to the "Haunted House" by a well-meaning youth worker from an inner city neighborhood. The youth worker had temporarily left the group while he went to pay for their entrance tickets. He had underestimated their ability to bring harm.

I ran up to the attackers and confronted them, demanding that they stop what they were doing. I began to push them away, which was met with, "Don't you touch me! You keep your hands off of me!" Their anger was turned toward me now. Another male leader from our group, Gordon Frank, also stepped in to help push them back. He was also met with shouts like, "Who do you think you are touching me?" Our involvement changed their focus. While the other leaders in our group gathered the kids together to check on the injured, Frank and I were able to draw the group of angry teens down a hillside and away from the students. The problem was now they were hitting Frank and me with their chain filled socks.

As I backed down the hill, I covered the sides of my head with my hands and received a number of blows to the back of my hands. I looked to my right and saw Frank was experiencing the same thing. Four of the students were hitting him and four were after me. In all the confusion, no one saw where we went. The other leaders in our group were focused on the injured and unaware of what was happening to Frank and me. The important thing was the angry teens were far enough away from my group and they were no longer a threat to them. Frank and I were all alone, down the hill and in the dark. This area of the parking lot was isolated and there were no other people around.

Confused by these actions, I kept asking the attackers, "Why are you doing this?" My question was only met with angry mostly indiscernible shouts. Occasionally I could hear them yelling about me touching them and I should not have put my hands on them. I did not know what was going to happen to Frank and me. I actually began to fear for our lives. But before the fear of dying got too strong, seemingly out of nowhere, appeared a man who seemed to be a little older and respected by the attackers. Later I learned he was not the leader who had brought them to the Haunted House, but who he was remains a mystery today.

Between blows from the socks, I looked at him and asked him if he would make them stop. He hesitated as if to say, "Why should I?" but then decided to listen to me. It worked and as quickly as it started, it was over. The attackers were gone. Frank and I looked at each other in disbelief about what had just happened. I expected him to be bleeding as he did me. But neither of us had any bleeding wounds. In fact, we weren't even in pain. All the hitting by the chained filled socks didn't even bruise the backs of our hands. We both felt like it was a miracle that we were unscathed.

We immediately went back to the line to assess the damage to our group. We had some youth in need of immediate medical attention, others not so bad, but everyone was upset. I led the most injured toward a first aid station inside the haunted house.

As we were waiting for help, we could hear the angry mob of teens had made it inside the haunted house and were now attacking the "actors" who were part of the haunted house. Dressed as goblins and stationed throughout the house, the "actors" were there to scare patrons as they passed by in the dark. They were now the recipients of blows from the socks filled with chains.

About then, law enforcement arrived at the first aid station. Apparently, we were not the first to be attacked by this group. The police had been called and were now on the scene, guns drawn and ready for action. The sheriff standing closest to me in the first aid station cocked his shotgun and said "let's go get 'em," Not wanting to be around if guns were going to be fired, I gathered up my injured and headed for the busses as fast as we could. We loaded everyone on the busses and headed back home to a local hospital, wounded and bleeding.

When we arrived back home, we sent the injured to the hospital and gathered the rest in a large room. It was hard for me to speak without being emotional, but through tears of emotion, I tried to communicate to this impressionable group of young men and women that they should not hate the ones who did this or judge all minorities and especially blacks because of what had just happened. This small group of angry teenagers did not represent the majority. With all my heart, I pleaded with my young students not to stereotype others because of these attacks, but to find and give forgiveness.

My hope was that this incident would not create a new generation of racially insensitive people filled with anger and bent toward stereotyping. The youth leader responsible for bringing the angry teens barely survived the night himself. There were no shots fired at the Haunted House and the teens were ushered back to the bus they had come in. The story I heard was that the youth leader and his assistant had to use force to get them off the bus once they arrived back at their neighborhood. I did not pursue any action against the teens and never heard anything about them again.

Chapter Sixteen

The Future

Where are we now as a nation? In the twenty-first century, we should not be talking about "their fight" against racism, but of "our fight."

As I said earlier, my sentiments about the "Salute" were way out of sync with my father and his friends in my hometown. Worse yet, strains of those same sentiments exist today among my peers, but with a little different twist. Cries of reverse racism pepper our dialogue today, with feelings of resentment toward the advances blacks have made in the job market, sometimes at the expense of a white person. Some feel "Equal Opportunity Employment" has gone too far and it is now the white worker who is being discriminated against. Some feel "Political Correctness" prevents a fair dialogue about many racial issues.

Some of my favorite editorial writers today can be found in the *Orange County Register*. Larry Elder, Thomas Sowell and Walter Williams are three I love to read. As black Americans they put a healthy perspective on the problems of an "entitlement" culture among some blacks and the ongoing racist attitudes by many whites today. They point out how this "entitlement mentality" only increases the feelings of victimization while removing motivation for betterment and how racism still exists creating a negative impact on society.

One thing for sure, the uniqueness of the plight of the black person from the days of slavery to the present will never be fully appreciated by whites or forgotten by blacks. The scar on our history and the ongoing social issues are a long way from being healed.

Will racism ever end? I doubt it. As long as we have differences, we humans will always find a way to hate. The only hope is for a reduction and that reduction comes through changed hearts. There is hope of less hate and more love and understanding, but we have a long way to go. Just one changed heart can and will help countless numbers of people.

Persons of every race can examine their hearts and determine how they can learn to respect all people and cull out any form of racism, overt or subtle, which may be in them. My friends like to talk about building bridges, relationship bridges, bridges designed to increase understanding and share life's values.

Realistically, there is nothing we can do to undo the horrible treatment of human beings which occurred in the past, but we can work toward making sure slavery never happens again and somehow mitigate the pain it has caused. Each of us could extend ourselves and partner with a person of a different ethnicity to learn about what their life is like. With God's help, hate can be replaced with love, mutual respect and understanding.

I think Smith's prayer from the medal stand is worth repeating.

"My prayer was for solidarity. A prayer of Hope, hope that we could unite as a people instead of being separatists in a country that is supposed to be one."

In many ways we are still a nation of separatists. I thought that maybe the outcome of the Civil Rights Movement would see us be a nation of Americans united for the common good of all Americans, and by extension, all humans in the world. Maturity is a word that comes to mind. Many Americans, people of all ethnicities, are immature in their attitudes toward those of a different race. A mature person is not threatened by anyone different. From my observations, there is a general uneasiness between blacks and whites. The suspicion is not gone. Blacks can be suspicious of the motives of a white person for either being overly nice or overly cold. Whites can be suspicious of blacks as to motives and a sense of entitlement. These problems are not just between blacks and whites in our multi-ethnic culture.

Politicians have not done much to help bring the maturity our country needs. In fact, they have created things which seem to emphasize differences. The idea of political correctness being achieved by adding a hyphen to our ethnicity has not achieved the harmony and respect that would indicate maturity. Love for our fellow man has been politicized. "Tolerance" has become the standard of dealing with differences. The idea of being tolerant is not what is needed today, it is not a big enough word to describe what needs to happen. Brotherhood is not something that should be mandated by law. We need to take politics out of the equation if we want to go beyond "tolerance" and reach maturity in race relations.

Eli Steele is a filmmaker and graduate student at Pepperdine University's School of Public Policy. He is developing a documentary on interracial Americans. I think Eli is on to something when talking about "identity politics," the politically correct way of categorizing minorities with labels that place race, ethnicity or religion before national identity. So much of this has contributed to the immaturity of America in regards to race relations. Steele is the father of two inter-racial children. The following is a summary of his view of identity politics. The full article is in appendix 5.

He believes his interracial children will find themselves at odds with America's politically correct "identity politics" when they grow up and become aware of our political system. He feels the interracial generation will be in the best position to point

America back to its "tradition of individualism."

"Most minorities today fall conveniently within categories such as African American, Chinese American or Mexican American. These labels arose during an era of political correctness that literally placed race, ethnicity or religion before national identity. Since the 1960s, minorities have found in their racial identity a preferential gateway into public and private institutions," he says.

He then asks an important question:

"Will such identity politics survive the interracial baby boom? Will new categories arise for the African German American or Chinese Latino American? Will a critical mass of inter-racials become an eclectic race in their own right? Or will they bypass the labels and embrace individualism?"

He regrets that in " identity politics" race is what matters not individual stories. In his opinion, identity politics has elevated racial identity to a place of social currency, "rewarded by preferences in college admissions, government contracts and employment." His children would do well in that game, but if they do they lose, along with their peers, the opportunity to "restore a weakened American legacy: the self-invented and self-made individual." He hopes they will be free to carve out their own identities.[26]

The mayoral race in September 2010 in Washington D.C. had an interesting twist. A twist which brings to light the complexity of race relations in local politics. Thomas Sowell, a Syndicated Columnist, shared this information about the election. The race pitted two black men against each other, the incumbent Mayor Adrian Fenty and Council Chairman Vincent Gray. He says that "few things have captured in microcosm what has gone so

---

26 Steele, Eli, "An interracial tipping point?" *Los Angeles Times*, September 21, 2010, A15.

painfully wrong, where racial issues are concerned" like this election.

Few things have captured in microcosm what has gone so painfully wrong, where racial issues are concerned, like the recent election for mayor of Washington, D.C. Mayor Adrian Fenty, under whom the murder rate has gone down and the school children's test scores have gone up, was resoundingly defeated for re-election.

Nor was Mayor Fenty simply a passive beneficiary of the rising test scores and falling murder rates. He appointed Michelle Rhee as head of the school system and backed her as she fought the teachers' union and fired large numbers of ineffective teachers—something considered impossible in most cities across the country. Mayor Fenty also appointed the city's chief of police, Cathy Lanier, who has cracked down on hoodlumism, as well as crime.

Either one of these achievements would made mayors local heroes in most other cities. Why then was he clobbered in the election? One key fact tells much of the story: Mayor Fenty received more than 70 percent of the white vote in Washington. His opponent received more than 80 percent of the black vote.

Both men are black. But the head of the school system that he appointed is Asian and the chief of police is a white woman. More than that, most of the teachers who were fired were black. There were also bitter complaints that black contractors did not get as many of the contracts for doing business with the city as they expected.

In short, the mayor appointed the best people he could find, instead of running a racial patronage system, as a black mayor of a city with a black majority is apparently expected to. He also didn't spend as much time schmoozing with the folks as was expected.

So what if he gave their children a better education and gave everybody a lower likelihood of being murdered? The mayor's faults were political faults. He did his job, produced results and thought that this should be enough to get him re-elected.

How did we reach the point where black voters put racial patronage and racial symbolism above the education of their children and the safety of everyone?

Sowell answers that question by explaining that programs like "war on poverty" under President Lyndon Johnson gave rise to a government-supported industry of race hustling. The tax-payer money available gave community activists every reason to hype racial resentments. Racial anger is the fuel that keeps the lucrative racket of race hustling going, according to Sowell.

Lyndon Johnson once said that it is not hard to do the right thing. What is hard is knowing what is right. We can give him credit for good intentions, so long as we remember what road is paved with good intentions.[27] You can read the full story in appendix 6.

The use of electronic media is a new way of keeping the tension going. Sending an e-mail is the new "water cooler joke" location. In the past, dirty and racist jokes were spread during work breaks in the office while co-workers gathered to get a drink of water. One person would say "Did you hear the latest..." and then proceed to tell a dirty joke or one laced with racist humor. Now these jokes are passed on through e-mails and sometimes attributed to a TV or movie star. The "Star" quality is intended to give it an air of authenticity. Usually a quick check of truthorfiction.com reveals the story to be false, but the damage is done. An ethnic stereotype or a hateful comment is now spreading through cyberspace.

---

27 Sowell, Thomas, "Race resentment racket." *The Orange County Register,* September 22, 2010, Local 9.

"Will writing about Evans and 'the Salute' change anything?" "Won't writing about it now after forty years just stir up trouble?" "Why can't we just let that rest," some may say. It has taken me over forty years to get a perspective on my experiences at San Jose State. Lee told his life story in 2006. The book is *The Last Protest: Lee Evans in Mexico City* by Frank Murphy. It is a great read, giving stirring accounts of Evan's journey to the gold medals in Mexico City. Smith and Carlos are thoughtful men and their opinions still valued. Smith and Carlos have both written their stories in the twenty-first century.

We all need to work hard at ferreting out the negative stereotypes from our upbringing. Everyone has the ongoing need to grow, mature and educate those around us. We need to strive not to pass the subtle and overt attitudes toward other races to our children. I hope my grandchildren will be more mature than my generation with regards to race and differences.

Many people find through spiritual conversion they can begin to treat others in a loving way. But whether an atheist, agnostic, Hindu, Buddhist, Muslim, humanist or Christian, we all should heed these truths:

...If we could change ourselves, the tendencies in the world would also change. As a man changes his own nature, so does the attitude of the world change towards him……We need not wait to see what others do.[28] —Ghandi

Jesus said, *"Love the Lord your God with all your heart and with all your soul and with all your mind and with all your strength. Love your neighbor as yourself."*[29]

"Hatred does not cease by hatred, but only by love; this is the eternal rule," Buddha.

---

28 The Collected Works of M.K. Ghandi, vol 13, Ch 153 General Knowledge About Health: 241.

29 The New International Version, Zondervan Bible Publishers, 1973.

Will you join me in praying for a new day of love, brotherhood and unity? Please turn to appendix 7 to read more about my personal spiritual journey and the basis for my life then and now.

Appendix 1
In their own words

Following is a very intriguing interview with Tommie Smith and Lee Evans in 1967. Dick Drake of *Track and Field News* did the interview. Reading it gives you a clear sense of where Smith and Evans were coming from and how talk of a boycott started which eventually led to the "Black Power" salute in the 1968 Games in Mexico City. Pay close attention to Drake's comments leading up to the interview.

This interview first appeared in the November 1967 issue of Track & Field News, Mountain View, CA. Drake was the Operation Manager for Track and Field News and is used with permission.

INTERVIEW INTRODUCTION by Dick Drake

On Sept. 3 during this year's World Student Games in Tokyo, a Japanese reporter asked Tommie Smith, "In the United States, are the Negroes now equal to the whites in the way they are treated?" His obvious answer was, "No". The American Negro sprinter was then asked, "What about the possibility of (U.S.) Negroes boycotting the 1968 Olympics?", a question probably prompted by comedian Dick Gregory's request—made at least partially in deference to the stripping of Muhammad Ali's world heavyweight boxing title—that such an act be considered by

Olympic prospects. Tommie's reply was, "Depending upon the situation, you cannot rule out the possibility that we (U.S.) Negro athletes might boycott the Olympic Games."

This was the first occasion that Tommie Smith had been asked to reflect upon his thoughts concerning a boycott—either publicly or privately. The only previous publicly circulated statement on the boycott question by any American track and field athlete came from Ralph Boston, who, while he expressed a belief that it would not serve any purpose, did not categorically deny the possibility of such a development.

The world's most prolific global record holder has since denied that he is actively leading or advocating a boycott and has rebuked the idea that any outside individual or group from the black ranks has approached him. Tommie has affirmed that any withdrawal of Negro athletes from the Mexico Olympics would primarily come as a result of discussions among the athletes themselves.

The whole matter was further blown out of proportion when it was learned that Tommie and teammate Lee Evans were members of the executive committee for the United Black Students for Action (UBSA) at San Jose State, whose organization sought equality in housing, membership in social groups and in athletics during the first week of school this fall.

Pressmen the world over rushed to their typewriters to picture Tommie as a militant Negro leader or as an athletic stooge for extremist black groups and promptly scorned the merits of a boycott. What he has said, in effect, is two-fold: (1) I am concerned about the problems facing my race here and now, and (2) the Negro athletes might conclude that boycotting the Olympics would be an effectual tool in our battle for racial equality. No one at this stage knows whether a boycott will be forthcoming, and neither Tommie nor Lee is willing to conjecture at this time as to the possibility that it would actually transpire.

Talk to them, and you'll learn that their desire to participate in the Games is intense. They would have perhaps more to gain by winning a gold medal than the next white guy. And so, you must come to the question, what is it they feel so strongly about that they would sacrifice considerable personal glory and why would they consider jeopardizing their track careers? Reams of copy have been devoted to the possibility of such a boycott— and much of it based on misinformation—but little of it has dealt with the question of WHY the blacks would forfeit an opportunity to compete in the world's most important athletic event that many of them have already devoted countless hours striving to reach.

Thus, I invited Tommie and Lee to my apartment to express into an unbiased tape-recorder their views through a series of questions which I had hoped would shed some light on the confusion which has ensued since Sept. 3 and would unearth some of the deep-seated feelings which might result in U.S. black athletes taking such an action as boycotting the Olympics.

The transcription that follows represents the opinions of two Negroes, who through personal insight, education, athletic achievement and world travel are becoming aware of the problems faced by the U.S. black people and who are motivated and prepared to accept the responsibility of sacrificing their own personal achievement for a cause (not necessarily athletic boycott) they believe would aid in the cause of racial equality. As two non-militant, non-extremist Negroes, they are simply verbalizing the feelings of resentment and dissatisfaction perhaps typical of many of their brothers. As two prominent Negro athletes, their opinions about the possibility and effectiveness of a boycott do not necessarily represent the attitudes or desires of other Olympic Negro hopefuls.

Tommie and Lee, of course, are no strangers to the world of track nuts. On the strength of their track exploits alone, there are few athletes whose names are better known to the casual track fan. Between them, they claim at least portions of eleven world records.

Tommie, now twenty-three and still a student at San Jose State though without further track eligibility, holds world records at 200-meters and 220-yards straightaway (19.5), 200-meters and 220-yards turn (20.0), and has marks pending in the 400-meters (44.5) and 440-yards (44.8) as well as indoor marks in the 400-meters and 440-yards (46.2). Both Tommie and Lee ran on their school's world record 800-meter and 880-yard relay (1:22.1) and on the U.S. national team that claims the world standard in the 1600-meter relay (2:59.6). They also ran on the San Jose State team that bettered the American standard in the mile relay (3:93.5).

Lee, three years younger and a junior in eligibility, ranked number one in the world last year in the quarter mile by T&FN. His 44.9 for 400-meters is equal second best of all-time. He had lost only to Tommie (in the world record 400/440) this year until injured in Europe. Neither has competed on an Olympic team though both have taken foreign tours with U.S. teams.

Because these pages are devoted to athletics, we must necessarily limit the discussion that developed to those aspects that at least indirectly relate to track and field. Both Tommie and Lee have read this report in its entirety and at least concur as to its factual content. Whether or not you agree with the merits of a U.S. Negro boycott of the 1968 Olympics, you should find the reasons that would motivate such an action revealing.

QUESTION: Has there been any single major event which has prompted the suggestion that Negroes boycott the Olympics? What role did the stripping of Muhammad Ali's boxing title and Dick Gregory's subsequent request that Negroes boycott the Games play in the current thinking?

EVANS: What Dick Gregory said doesn't have much to do

with what I feel. I think that many Negroes are becoming aware of what's happening. In high school, I didn't know what was coming off, but in college I have become aware and concerned. Of course, what they did to Ali affects my opinion. I just don't dig some of the things that are happening.

QUESTION: What is the objective of such a movement? What do you and others hope can be achieved with a boycott? Do you think any concrete results can be achieved? Or is it merely symbolic?

EVANS: In terms of what I have put into the sport, I think that I will be really hurt, But, then you begin thinking about what the Negro has been going through in this country. When you come back from the Olympics with a gold medal, you might be high on the hog for a month, but after that you would be just another guy. Look at Bob Richards on TV. Why don't they have Bob Hayes or Henry Carr advertising on TV? If they had them advertising Wheaties, some of the white people in the south might stop purchasing their product. As for myself, I would be most interested in seeing something done now so that things would be different by the 1972 Olympics.

SMITH: There have been a lot of marches, protests and sit-ins on the situation of Negro ostracism in the U.S. And I don't think that this boycott of the Olympics would stop the problem, but I think people will see that we will not sit on our haunches and take this sort of stuff. We are a race of proud people and want to be treated as such. Our goal would not be to just improve conditions for ourselves and teammates, but to improve things for the entire Negro community.

You must regard this suggestion as only another step in a series of movements. Maybe discrimination won't stop in the next ten years but it will represent another important development. As far as being spit on, being stepped on, being bitten by dogs, the first dog that bites me I'm going to bite back. We're not going to wait for the white man to think of something else to do against us—as in politics which is currently working against us. And it doesn't do any good to put an Uncle Tom into high position. I have worked for a long time for the Olympics, and I would hate to lose all that. But I think that boycotting the Olympics for a good cause is strong enough reason not to compete.

EVANS: I think Negroes are realizing that the white man doesn't go by his own rules, such as in civil rights. To the extent that I think things would be different for the American Negro by 1972, I am willing to consider boycotting. We are men first and athletes second. Professional athletes are even quitting now because of prejudice.

QUESTION: What prompted you, Tommie, to comment about the possibility of a boycott in Japan?

SMITH: My comments in Japan came as a result of quite a bit of listening and reading and thinking for myself. The reporter asked me about the possibility of a boycott. I told him that there is a chance, and the reason was literally because of the ostracism of the U.S. Negro. I had made no comment prior to then. I was not motivated to comment as the result of anything Ralph Boston or Dick Gregory had said.

QUESTION: Is there any group or individual behind the proposal for a boycott?

SMITH: I couldn't say, but no one has approached me. It's up to the Negro athletes to decide, and we have not met as a group to discuss the boycott. There will be a Black Youth Conference in Los Angeles on November 23, on which occasion we will discuss the possibilities with athletes from other sports as well. This meeting will not include all the major track and field athletes, but I think we will draw a lot of conclusions. Again, I'm not advocating the boycott.

QUESTION: How serious is the possibility of a boycott?

What are the chances that it will transpire?

EVANS: There is a chance it will happen. But it just depends. The guys in California would give up the opportunity to compete; they'd hate to but then you've got to do something. But then there are the athletes from the other forty-nine states. I really want to go to the Olympics, but I'll pass it up if I have to—for a just cause.

SMITH: I think a close enough decision will develop at this meeting to know what will happen.

EVANS: If everyone is willing to do it, I'm sure we're going to do it.

QUESTION: Of the Negro athletes you've talked with, what percent would you say support or would support a boycott?

EVANS: You have to go to different sections of the country. I think in California, it would be 75 percent right now. But if you go to the south or southwest these are the guys who are catching the most hell in the streets and they just don't understand the need for a boycott. The schools in the south simply aren't the same as in the west. So, these guys aren't aware of what's happening. The schools don't get them to thinking, and the guys don't read about the problems. They don't think about their jobs and what their parents were doing. They're just thinking about themselves and what the Olympics would mean.

SMITH: Some of these guys from the south look at you funny. But look at it this way. How would you like it if you said something in California and you got back to your home in the south to find a double barrel shotgun sticking in your front door? I think the guys are more afraid than anything.

QUESTION: What has motivated your current activist roles?

SMITH: Thinking.

EVANS: Thinking.

SMITH: Like Lee says, as a senior in high school I looked upon my ability as something no one else had, and looking at this ability alone I neglected to realize there might be something else to life than just track. It's only been in the last two years that I have begun to see that there are problems, and that I must learn to cope with them. And I'm starting by looking at myself.

QUESTION: How have your opinions altered in the past six weeks since going on record about all this?

SMITH: It has forced me to read and think about the problems of this day and age—even more than six months ago. If this individual in Japan would not have asked me about the possibility of a boycott in 1968, I might not have begun really thinking about this specific suggestion. All of a sudden something suddenly flashed into my mind. Is there something to it? What is this individual asking me? Am I going to take the ostracism I'm taking now, or if this Japanese knew this, where did it come from?

QUESTION: Could you give up athletics tomorrow?

SMITH: I would give up athletics tomorrow if the cause were strong enough. I would give up athletics in a minute to die for my people.

QUESTION: What about the challenges that you, Tom, have lost your humility with respect to what athletics has given you? What is your reaction to columns such as the one by Jim Murray of the *Los Angeles Times* wherein he called you a downy-cheeked kid who has an exaggerated opinion of his own athletic importance?

SMITH: There are some people who are pen happy. As far as Murray's standpoint, I think he is looking at it all on a narrow line and not objectively. I don't think most writers are like this, but Murray is. Because he has said something about me that wasn't true. One quotation in particular bothered me, and that was that I was advocating a boycott. And then there were a lot of smaller things that added up to one big lie. To the average individual, it made me look like something lower than a rat.

EVANS: It made Tommie look like militant Tommie. As soon as you become aware of what is happening to your people, you are considered militant. UBSA is considered a militant group because we got things done on the campus. That campus is a lot better now. And other campuses could be as well if they'd just do something.

QUESTION: Why boycott only the Olympics? Why single them out for boycotting, while continuing to compete for a school which has been charged with discrimination and in a country where it exists?

EVANS: The school is just a part of this country. So, I think we should hit at the top. And this country—I can't dig why the U.S. voted to permit South Africa to compete in the Olympics. That was what I was told, anyway. I'm definitely going to discuss this matter at this conference. They send this cat Paul Nash to run here in the U.S. If I went to South Africa, they wouldn't let me run in no damn meet with Paul Nash. But he can come here and run with us. I'm supposed to be an American, but I'm not treated as one.

Coach Stan Wright wrote Tommie a letter telling him that he should consider himself an American first, a Negro second. But nobody else considers me an American first. You read any kind of book or magazine. Even *Track & Field News* says Negro Stan Wright. The first thing you're told or see is that you're a Negro, but still you're supposed to be an American. If you publish a picture, people can look at it and tell if you're Negro. So, you don't have to mention it.

SMITH: What kind of logic is this to let Paul Nash come to America to compete for South Africa. Lee or (Ralph) Boston or myself cannot go as Americans to compete in South Africa. Now, if we are Americans, if (Jim) Ryun and I are both Americans, why can't I go to South Africa and compete in the same meets? If we can't go there, why can they come here?

EVANS: This is where you can hit them the hardest. This is one of the major areas where the U.S. gets its international sports propaganda. The Olympics are a big thing, and the press help to create this. So, if the people want us Negroes to help promote U.S. sports propaganda, they can help us too.

SMITH: Why should we boycott the Olympics instead of the meets at our college? A good percentage of the Negroes are in college because of a scholarship. Now, if we discontinue athletics, the scholarship almost means our lives to us. I got my education through a scholarship. If I had discontinued competition, it would have meant that my scholarship would have been taken away. Therefore, I wouldn't have gotten an education and gotten as far as I have, and so I wouldn't know what I'm talking about. Education is a prelude to a later advancement in life: knowledge. Therefore, unless you have the financial background, discontinuing athletics wouldn't be advantageous to any cause. You have less to lose and more to gain by boycotting the Olympics than at San Jose State—because this is the way you have hit the hardest.

QUESTION: When did you sense a change in your opinions?

SMITH: It began when I started walking and thinking I am a Negro. I wish I could give you a definite date. I said, here's a white man, I'm a Negro. He can walk into this store, why can't I? It really started last semester, and then Tokyo helped. I took a class in black leadership; it started me to thinking. What the hell is going on in the U.S.? I'm a human. What kind of rights do I have? What kind of rights don't I have? Why can't I have these rights?

EVANS: I started reading. That's what got me to thinking.

QUESTION: Have you experienced any blatant or subtle discrimination on international track teams?

EVANS: [Lee related two incidences concerning John Carlos and George Anderson at the US-Commonwealth meet which he felt were either the result of misunderstandings or were sufficiently remedied so as not to be classifiable as acts of discrimination.] But we were going to boycott that meet as a Negro block if they didn't use the first four finishers in the American women's 100-yard dash at the AAU in the relay—who all happened to be Negroes. They intended to substitute Dee DeBusk for Mattiline Render. But as it turned out, Barbara Farrell got injured, so both Dee and Mattiline got to run. And that saved the situation.

QUESTION: How do you professors at San Jose State regard you in general?

EVANS: They know us as the fastest nigger on campus. They only talk to us because we're athletes. They don't talk to the next Negro who passes by.

SMITH: Often, they say congratulations to me. I say, "Thank you. What did I do?" I say, "On my marriage or on a test?" And they say, "No, on your world record." They never talk about my marriage or academics.

EVANS: You are a fast nigger. They don't say nigger but that's what—they mean.

SMITH: There's one coach who doesn't think that the Negroes can have any sentimental value. And when he looks at you, he regards you only as an athlete. And he tries to find the easiest classes for you so you can get through college. Now, how the hell are you going to get an education with fifteen units of badminton?

EVANS: You get a sheet from them that says what it takes to get through college.

SMITH: I'm taking a couple of courses that I have no interest in. But I have to take them. Look at ROTC, for example. As a result of my lack of interest, I'm not getting good grades. Why should I go to Viet Nam and fight for this country and come back when my equality will still be half taken away? If I could come back here just like my white friends, I'd be happy to be a lieutenant in the Army.

The following statements by Tommie and Lee were issued to the press at large, and will serve as their concluding comments to this interview.

EVANS: My own position on a boycott is this: the Olympics are something that I have dreamed of participating in ever since I first learned to run. This does not, however, mean participation at any price. And my own manhood is one of the prices that I am not willing to pay. A second and more important price that I am not under any circumstances willing to pay is that of slamming a potential door to freedom in the face of black people. If this door can be opened by my not participating, then I will not participate.

SMITH: I want to clarify several points that I am alleged to have made at a recent speaking engagement in Lemoore, California. Several points that I made were taken completely out of context. The Olympic Games are and always have been of extreme importance and significance to me. I did make the statement that I would give my right arm to participate and win a gold medal, but it was taken out of context as I am not willing to sacrifice the basic dignity of my people to participate in the Games.

I am quite willing not only to give up participation in the Games but my life as well if necessary to open a door by which the oppression and injustices suffered by black people in the U.S. might be alleviated. If the group decision is to boycott, I will participate wholeheartedly.

Appendix 2

This was a BBC Report published on October 17, 1968. This gives insight into what was being reported to the world immediately after the salute.

Two black American athletes have made history at the Mexico Olympics by staging a silent protest against racial discrimination.

Tommie Smith and John Carlos, gold and bronze medalists in the 200m, stood with their heads bowed and a black-gloved hand raised as the American National Anthem played during the victory ceremony. The pair both wore black socks and no shoes and Smith wore a black scarf around his neck. They were demonstrating against continuing racial discrimination of black people in the United States.

As they left the podium at the end of the ceremony they were booed by many in the crowd.

At a press conference after the event Tommie Smith, who holds seven world records, said: "If I win I am an American, not a black American. But if I did something bad then they would say 'a Negro.' We are black and we are proud of being black. Black America will understand what we did tonight." Smith said he had raised his right fist to represent black power in America, while Carlos raised his left fist to represent black unity. Together they formed an arch of unity and power. He said the black scarf represented black pride and the black socks with no shoes stood for black poverty in racist America. Within a couple of hours the actions of the two Americans were being condemned by the International Olympic Committee. A spokesperson for the organization said it was "a deliberate and violent breach of the fundamental principles of the Olympic spirit." It is widely expected the two will be expelled from the Olympic village and sent back to the U.S.

In September last year Tommie Smith, a student at San Jose State university in California, told reporters that black members of the American Olympic team were considering a total boycott of the 1968 games.

He said: "It is very discouraging to be in a team with white athletes. On the track you are Tommie Smith, the fastest man in the world, but once you are in the dressing rooms you are nothing more than a dirty Negro." The boycott had been the idea of professor of sociology at San Jose State University, and friend of Tommie Smith, Harry Edwards. Professor Edwards set up the Olympic Project for Human Rights (OPHR) and appealed to all black American athletes to boycott the games to demonstrate to the world that the civil rights movement in the U.S. had not gone far enough. He told black Americans they should refuse "to be utilized as 'performing animals' in the games."

Although the boycott never materialized the OPHR gained much support from black athletes around the world.

Appendix 3

This interview was conducted by American sports writer Dave Zirin on November 1, 2003 and was published in Z Magazine in December 2003. Used with permission.

Thirty-five years ago, John Carlos became one half of perhaps the most famous (or infamous) moment in Olympic history. After winning the bronze medal in the 200 meter dash, he and gold medalist Tommy Smith, raised their black glove clad fists in a display of "black power." It was a moment that defined the revolutionary spirit and defiance of a generation. Now as the 35th anniversary of that moment passes with nary a word, John Carlos talks about those turbulent times.

DZ: Many call that period of the 1960s, the revolt of the black athlete. Why?

JC: I think *Sports Illustrated* started that phrase. I don't think of it as the revolt of the black athlete at all. It was the revolt of the black men. Athletics was my occupation. I didn't do what I did as an athlete. I raised my voice in protest as a man. I was fortunate enough to grow up in the era of Dr. King, of Paul Robeson, of baseball players like Jackie Robinson and Roy Campanella who would come into my dad's shop on 142nd street and Lennox in Harlem. I could see how they were treated as black athletes. I would ask myself, why is this happening? Racism meant that none of us could truly have our day in the sun. Without education, housing, and employment, we would lose what I call "family hood." If you can't give your wife or son or daughter what they need to live, after a while you try to escape who you are. That's why people turn to drugs and why our communities have been destroyed. And that's why there was a revolt.

DZ: When you woke up that morning in 1968, did you know you were going to make your historic gesture on the medal stand or was it spontaneous?

JC: It was in my head the whole year. We first tried to have a boycott [to get all Black athletes to boycott the Olympics] but not everyone was down with that plan. A lot of the athletes thought that winning medals would supersede or protect them from racism. But even if you won the medal it ain't going to save your momma. It ain't going to save your sister or children. It might give you fifteen minutes of fame, but what about the rest of your life? I'm not saying they didn't have the right to follow their dreams, but to me the medal was nothing but the carrot on a stick.

DZ: At the last track meet before the Olympics, we left it that every man would do his own thing. You had to choose which side of the fence you were on. You had to say, "I'm for racism or I'm against racism."

JC: We stated we were going to do something. But Tommie and I didn't know what we were going to do until we got into the tunnel [on the way to the race]. We had gloves, black shirts and beads. And we decided in that tunnel that if we were going to go out on that stand, we were going to go out barefooted.

DZ: Why Barefooted?

JC: We wanted the world to know that in Mississippi, Alabama, Tennessee, South Central Los Angeles, Chicago, that people were still walking back and forth in poverty without even the necessary clothes to live. We have kids that don't have shoes even today. It's not like the powers that be can't do it provide these things. They can send a space ship to the moon, or send a probe to Mars, yet they can't give shoes? They can't give health care? I'm just not naive enough to accept that.

DZ: Why did you wear beads on the medal stand?

JC: The beads were for those individuals that were lynched, or killed that no one said a prayer for, that were hung tarred. It was for those thrown off the side of the boats in the middle passage. All that was in my mind. We didn't come up there with any bombs. We were trying to wake the country up and wake the world up too.

DZ: How did your life change when you took that step onto the podium?

JC: My life changed prior to the podium, I used to break into freight trains by Yankee Stadium when I was young. Then I changed when I realized I was a force in track and field. I realized I didn't have to break into freight trains. I wanted to wake up the people who work and run the trains so they can seize what they deserve. It's like these supermarkets in Southern California that are on strike. They always have extra milk and they throw it in the river or dump it the garbage even though there are people without milk. They say we can't give it to you so we would rather throw it away. Something is very wrong. Realizing that changed me long before 1968.

DZ: What kind of harassment did you face back home?

JC: I was with Dr. King ten days before he died. He told me he was sent a letter that said there was a bullet with his name on it. I remember looking in his eyes to see if there was any fear, and there was none. He didn't have any fear. He had love and that in itself changed my life in terms how I would go into battle. I would never have fear for my opponent, but love for the people I was fighting for. That's why if you look at the picture [of the raised fist] Tommy has his jacket zipped up, and [silver medalist] Peter Norman has his jacket zipped up, but mine was open. I was representing shift workers, blue-collar people, and the underdogs. That's why my shirt was open. Those are the people whose contributions to society are so important but don't get recognized.

DZ: What kind of support did you receive when you came home?

JC: There was pride but only from the less fortunate. What could they do but show their pride? But we had black businessmen, we had black political caucuses, and they never embraced Tommie Smith or John Carlos. When my wife took her life; 1977 and they never said, let me help.

DZ: What role did you being outcast have on your wife taking her own life?

JC: It played a huge role. We were under tremendous economic stress. I took any job I could find. I wasn't too proud. Menial jobs, security jobs, gardener, caretaker, whatever I could do to try to make ends meet. We had four children, and some nights I would have to chop up our furniture and put it in the fireplace to stay warm. I was the bad guy, the two headed dragon-spitting fire. It meant we were alone.

DZ: Many people say athletes should just play and not be heard. What do you say to that?

JC: Those people should put all their millions of dollars together and make a factory that builds athlete-robots. Athletes are human beings. We have feelings too. How can you ask someone to live in the world, to exist in the world, and not have something to say about injustice?

DZ: What message do you have to the new generation of

athletes hitting the world stage?

JC: First of all athletes black/red/brown/yellow and white need to do some research on their history; their own personal family They need to find out how many people in their family were maimed in a war. They need to find out how hard their ancestors had to work. They need to uncloud their minds with the materialism and the money and study their history. And then they need to speak up. You got to step up to society when it's letting all its people down.

DZ: As you look at the world today, do you think athletes and all people still need to speak out and take a stand?

JC: Yes, because so much is the same as it was in 1968 especially in terms of race relations. I think things are just more cosmetically disguised. Look at Mississippi, or Alabama. It hasn't changed from back in the day. Look at the city of Memphis and you still see blight up and down. You can still see the despair and the dope. Look at the police rolling up and putting twenty-nine bullets in a person in the hallway, or sticking a plunger up a man's rectum, or Texas where they dragged that man by the neck from the bumper of a truck. How is that not just the same as a lynching?

DZ: Do you feel like you are being embraced now after all these years?

JC: I don't feel embraced, I feel like a survivor, like I survived cancer. It's like if you are sick and no one wants to be around you, and when you're well everyone who thought you would go down for good doesn't even want to make eye contact. It was almost like we were on a deserted island. That's where Tommy Smith and John Carlos were. But we survived.

Appendix 4
Klarman's complete article
The Civil Rights Trap

"It is difficult to ask historically disadvantaged minority groups to be patient in waiting for full recognition of their constitutional rights. Thurgood Marshall, the great NAACP organizer and litigator, was asked after Brown vs. Board of Education whether, in light of threatened violence and school closures in the South (in the 1950s), he would have been 'well advised to let things move along gradually for a while.' Marshall responded that he did indeed believe in gradualism, but 'I also believe that 90-odd-years [the time elapsed since the Emancipation Proclamation] is pretty gradual.'

"Historically, American presidents have rarely gotten far ahead of public opinion on civil rights issues, and the few times they have, they've paid a substantial price for doing so.

"President Lincoln, known to history as the Great Emancipator, was a relative latecomer to the abolitionist cause. It was, in the end, battlefield losses during the Civil War that forced him, almost as an act of desperation, to free slaves in order to undermine the Confederate labor supply and strengthen Union military forces. The Emancipation Proclamation was so unpopular in parts of the North that it cost Republicans dozens of congressional seats as well as control of some Northern state legislatures in the fall of 1862.

"African American voters ended their decades-long loyalty to the Republican Party in the 1930s because President Franklin D. Roosevelt generally included blacks in the assistance offered by his New Deal. But even then, Roosevelt steadfastly refused to support federal anti-lynching and anti-poll tax legislation during his more than three terms in office. Why? Because the white South remained a vital component of the political coalition that had elected him. Eventually, Roosevelt issued an executive order barring racial discrimination by government war contractors, but only because he was desperate to avoid a threatened march on Washington by 100,000 African American protestors as the nation hovered on the brink of World War II.

"In 1948, President Truman issued landmark executive orders desegregating the federal military and civil service. But he did so only after advisers warned him, following the disastrous 1946 off-year congressional elections, that his only chance of reelection was taking a disproportionate share of the African American vote in the North. Truman ended up winning two-thirds of the black vote, and without it he would not have been reelected president.

"During the first two years of his presidency, John F. Kennedy refused to support civil rights legislation, which would have alienated the Southern Democrats who had proved vital to his election in 1960 and whom he was likely to need again in 1964. Kennedy even declined to fulfill his campaign promise to eliminate racial discrimination in federally subsidized housing 'with the stroke of a pen,' leading civil rights critics to deluge the White House with ballpoint pens in their 'Ink for Jack' campaign.

"It was only the momentous street demonstrations in Birmingham, Ala., and other Southern cities in the spring of 1963 that prompted Kennedy to act on civil rights. After opinion polls found that the percentage of Americans ranking civil rights as the nation's No. 1 priority had increased to 52% from 4%, Kennedy went on national television to announce that civil

rights was a 'moral issue as old as the Scriptures and as clear as the American Constitution.' That summer, the administration introduced groundbreaking civil rights legislation, which was enacted into law the following year."

Michael Klarman is a professor at Harvard Law School and the author of *From Jim Crow to Civil Rights*, which won the 2005 Bancroft Prize.

Appendix 5
Eli Steele's complete article
An interracial tipping point?

Eli Steele is a filmmaker and graduate student at Pepperdine University's School of Public Policy. He is developing a documentary on interracial Americans. I think Eli is on to something when talking about "identity politics." So much of this has contributed to the immaturity of America in regards to race relations. He is the father of two inter-racial children. The following is another version of identity politics.

The day will arrive when this interracial generation reaches political consciousness and finds itself at odds with America's divisive identity politics. Of all Americans, they represent the best opportunity to end these politics and point America back to its tradition of individualism.

Most minorities today fall conveniently within categories such as African American, Chinese American or Mexican American. These labels arose during an era of political correctness that literally placed race, ethnicity or religion before national identity. Since the 1960s, minorities have found in their racial identity a preferential gateway into public and private institutions.

Will such identity politics survive the interracial baby boom? Will new categories arise for the African German American or

Chinese Latino American? Will a critical mass of inter-racials become an eclectic race in their own right? Or will they bypass the labels and embrace individualism?

Jack and June will grow up hearing stories of their ancestors' struggles, triumphs and defeats. They will learn how each forebear's unique journey converges in their blood, giving them no easy allegiance to a single race. Individuals rather than tribes will form the foundation for their individuality.

Then one day a stranger will stare into their faces, unable to deduce a single race in the mix of features: "What are you?" If they are anything like I was when I was growing up, they will begin with their family history, only to be asked again, "But, what are you?" In the age of identity politics, it is not stories but race that matters.

Jack and June may have a hard row to hoe. Identity politics have made racial identity a social currency, rewarded by preferences in college admissions, government contracts and employment. Jack and June have the bloodlines to win preferences. But if they do, they enter into a world where no choice is clean-cut. Do they join the black, Jewish or Latino organizations—or all of them? Do they publicly cultivate one racial identity while privately living free of such categories with family and friends? Or do they come to the conclusion that identity politics cannot offer anything but the pretense of racial purity?

And then the ultimate irony: Jack and June are naturally more diverse than any amount of social engineering in neighborhoods, schools or offices can achieve. They are creations of a high humanism: the love of their parents, grandparents and great-great grandparents. Jack and June are the result that social engineering—integration, inclusion and diversity—often fails to achieve.

My hope is that my children and their peers will restore a weakened American legacy: the self-invented and self-made individual. If they do, they will be free, as their ancestors were, to carve out identities and contribute to an already rich heritage for future generations. (*L.A. times*, September 21, 2010.)

Appendix 6

Thomas Sowell's complete article

Race Resentment Racket

Few things have captured in microcosm what has gone so painfully wrong, where racial issues are concerned, like the recent election for mayor of Washington, D.C. Mayor Adrian Fenty, under whom the murder rate has gone down and the school children's test scores have gone up, was resoundingly defeated for re-election.

Nor was Mayor Fenty simply a passive beneficiary of the rising test scores and falling murder rates. He appointed Michelle Rhee as head of the school system and backed her as she fought the teachers' union and fired large numbers of ineffective teachers—something considered impossible in most cities across the country. Mayor Fenty also appointed the city's chief of police, Cathy Lanier, who has cracked down on hoodlumism, as well as crime.

Either one of these achievements would made mayors local heroes in most other cities. Why then was he clobbered in the election? One key fact tells much of the story: Mayor Fenty received more than 70 percent of the white vote in Washington. His opponent received more than 80 percent of the black vote.

Both men are black. But the head of the school system that he appointed is Asian and the chief of police is a white woman. More than that, most of the teachers who were fired were black. There were also bitter complaints that black contractors did not get as many of the contracts for doing business with the city as they expected.

In short, the mayor appointed the best people he could find, instead of running a racial patronage system, as a black mayor of a city with a black majority is apparently expected to. He also didn't spend as much time schmoozing with the folks as was expected.

So what if he gave their children a better education and gave everybody a lower likelihood of being murdered? The mayor's faults were political faults. He did his job, produced results and thought that this should be enough to get him re-elected.

How did we reach the point where black voters put racial patronage and racial symbolism above the education of their children and the safety of everyone?

There are many reasons but the trend is ominous. One key factor was the creation, back in the 1960s, of a whole government-supported industry of race hustling.

President Lyndon Johnson's "war on poverty"— a war that we have lost, by the way— bankrolled all kinds of local "leaders" and organizations with the taxpayers' money, in the name of community "participation" in shaping the policies of government.

These "leaders" and community activists have had every reason to hype racial resentments and to make issues "us" against "them."

One of the largely untold stories of our time has been the story of how ACORN, Jesse Jackson and other community activists have been able to transfer billions of dollars from banks to their own organizations' causes, with the aid of the federal government, exemplified by the Community Reinvestment Act and its sequels.

Racial anger and racial resentments are the fuel that keeps this lucrative racket going. How surprised should anyone be that community activist groups have used Mau Mau disruptions in banks and harassed both business and government officials in their homes?

Lyndon Johnson once said that it is not hard to do the right thing. What is hard is knowing what is right. We can give him credit for good intentions, so long as we remember what road is paved with good intentions.

Appendix 7
My Spiritual Journey

My spiritual journey started in 1964. It was during that time that I first started to read the Bible and understand the message Jesus was teaching. Because of this journey, I asked Lee to help me. I would like to share that journey.

With the help of some very good friends, I began to see what it really meant to be a Christian. Based on what I had been taught up to that point in my life, like many, I was confused about the true meaning of Christianity.

I was a member of a denominational church as a child and into my teen years. I had the impression that God judged us for eternal life based on two standards—the good things we did and the bad things we did not do. I was good on both those scales. In fact, I thought if God graded on a curve, the more bad things my friends did, the better off I was with God by comparison. I was a self-righteous person. Creating my on righteousness was not easy, but I felt pretty good about where I stood with God.

My life changed when I began to study the Bible and listen to the words of Jesus. You can only imagine the relief I felt when I fully understood God's plan, not Jim's plan. I had perverted the truth to the point of making life a burden, not joyful. I was growing tired of the game I was playing with God. It is hard to keep up the act 24/7.

What did I learn? First I learned that I was separated from God because of sin. I had inherited a sin nature at birth due to a long history of mankind rebelling against the Creator of the World and all of life. I came to understand there was nothing I could do within me to please God or earn his favor. I also learned I was already at rock bottom and so there was nothing I could do that was bad enough to make it any worse than it already was. There was no scale. Everyone was in the same boat. It was not easy for a self-righteous person to come to accept this truth. I wanted to earn it myself.

Next I learned that God did not leave us without hope. From the very beginning of time He has provided a way for man to regain what was lost through sin. I did not have to remain separated from Him and hopeless. And I did not have to create my own salvation through my own works. For the first time I understood that Jesus' death on the cross meant something. His death was providing me a way to reconnect with the Creator. The change came the night I gave myself to Jesus and accepted His offer of righteousness through His death and shedding of His blood.

I was off the self-righteous treadmill and living in God's grace. My life's purpose became clear—"proclaim the Glory of God and the salvation provided through faith in Jesus." I started confessing Him as my savior, much to the surprise of my friends. Before this, my life's purpose was to proclaim Jim. I wanted all that life had to offer for myself. I wanted all the glory to go to me.

My heart was changed. I experienced new birth, a spiritual birth. I stared reading the Bible every day. It was spiritual food for my soul. God's spirit came into my life, helping me understand things I never knew before. I saw life clearly and the path I was to follow. I learned what I experienced was available for anyone and everyone. I believe this new life and new heart is the way to learn how to love all men and to overcome the innate racism monster we all have. It has been through Christ I learned to overcome my inborn racism and instead have chosen to really love people—regardless of their race.

The reconciliation that God has brought to us through Christ can be brought between races of people with changed hearts through faith in Jesus. This is the only solution to the problem of hatred we face in the World today.

There are several key verses in the New Testament to guide us into understanding God's gift of life through faith in His son.

Romans 6:23 says: "For the wages of sin is death, but the gift of God is eternal life in Christ Jesus our Lord."

Romans 3:22-23 says: "This righteousness from God comes through faith in Jesus Christ to all who believe. There is no difference, for all have sinned and fall short of the glory of God and are justified freely by his grace through the redemption that came by Christ Jesus." Understanding this was the first step to healing for me.

John 1:10-13 says: "He [Jesus] was in the world, and though the world was made through him, the world did not recognize him. He came to that which was his own, but his own did not receive him. Yet to all who received him, to those who believed in his name, he have the right to become children of God— children born not of a natural descent, nor of human decision or a husband's will, but born of God."

Becoming a child of God is something given to me, not something I earned or deserved. It was a gift of God.

Ephesians 2:8-10: "For it is by Grace you have been saved, through faith-and this not from yourselves, it is the gift of God-not by works, so that no one can boast. For we are God's workmanship; created in Christ Jesus to do good works, which God prepared in advance for us to do."

I was free now to do good works, but not for salvation. I could no longer boast that I was the one earning God's favor. He gave me new life and a new purpose. The new life and new purpose has motivated me all my life. I would love to answer any questions about this.

The first verse I memorized was John 14:6, "Jesus said, I am the way, the truth and the life. No one comes to the Father except through me."

A renewed heart is God's way to real reconciliation.

Appendix 8
More about finding my way to San Jose

Following is a little more information about my evolution as a runner. I ran the mile competitively for six years, running in a total of sixty-five races. I had the good fortune of running during one of Track and Field's greatest eras. I will always be thankful for the God-given ability to run.

I won many races in dual meets over the next four years, but never any gold medals in championship meets. Competing in the mile run for two years of high school at Escondido High School in Escondido, California and two years of community college track at Palomar College in San Marcos, California netted me seven league, conference or state runner-up medals. I am known as "Runner-up" to one of my former coaches.

This was not particularly disappointing because the runners who beat me were quality runners. My junior year in high school, I placed 2nd in the Metro League finals mile to Hilltop High School senior John Link. This was my first year running the mile. I was beginning to understand the dedication required to be successful in the mile, but was inexperienced and still too immature physically to beat an older more experienced runner like Link. Link went on to run a 4:02 mile for USC. My best time was 4:32.2, a time that broke the existing Escondido High

School record.

Over the summer I trained hard for my senior year. I continued the two a day running schedule I started as a freshman, beginning each day with a five mile run. At the start of the season, I had great hopes of being Metro League champion now that Link had graduated. However, a young runner named Tim Danielson from Chula Vista High School arrived on the scene. Tim was coming into his own as a runner and left me in second place in the Metro League meet again. Tim won the county championships that year running 4:08 and went on to become the second high school runner to break four minutes in the mile his senior year. My best in high school was 4:19.2, good enough for 4th in San Diego County.

At Palomar College, my skill in running the mile improved greatly under first year coach Larry Knuth. Knuth taught my teammate Dave Funderburk and me about the success that comes through hard work. In 1966, Funderburk and I finished 1-2 in the Pacific Southwest Conference meet. In the Southern California JC Finals meet at Citrus College in Azusa, California the next week, Funderburk and I finished one-two in the mile, respectively, running 4:13.7 and 4:14.8. The one-two finish earned us a chance to compete in the California Junior College State Championships in Modesto, California. For two freshmen, a 1-2 finish in the Southern California Meet was a bit of an upset, especially since our coach—Knuth—was a twenty-four-year-old rookie in the coaching profession. At the State meet, Funderburk took third and I finished fourth. It was a successful year for both of us as runners and for Knuth as a coach.

The 1-2 finish at the Southern Cal meet prompted Knuth to say "To me, this was like Palomar gaining a bid to the Junior College Rose Bowl.... It was one of my biggest thrills as a coach."

As a college sophomore I continued to have success, winning

our conference mile and half-mile championships. Competing in the So. Cal. J C Mile Finals in San Diego's Balboa Stadium I placed 2nd again, losing in the last one hundred yards to Paul Robison of Santa Monica College. This loss and the reward of another silver medal was surprising since I thought I had the race won only to have Robison out sprint me in the last one hundred yards to finish in 4:09.2 to my 4:09.9. My goal of breaking the string of silver medals was broken.

For the second year, I traveled to Modesto, California for the Junior College State Championships. The previous year's champion was a twenty-five-year-old from England; Neil Duggan was back as a sophomore, running for Alan Hancock Junior College in Santa Maria, California. Duggan had experience in International competition and had already run faster than four minutes in the mile. I gave my best effort only to finish second one more time at 4:13 to the experienced Duggan at 4:12. I added another silver to my collection of medals.

Even though I had very few gold medals, my best time in the mile gave me options for the next level of education and competition. I received my Associate of Arts degree from Palomar College and was now ready to transfer to a four-year school. Getting the A.A. degree was not easy. In fact, I almost lost my options for the future with one semester of bad grades. In the fall of 1966, I continued to take Pre-Dental classes, feeling I would please my father by becoming a dentist like him. The idea was I would take over his practice some day in the future. The problem was I did not have the kind of mind that did well with physics and qualitative analysis; two prerequisites to dentistry. That combined with bad study habits and immaturity, I nearly failed several of my fall classes and would have not been eligible to run in the spring.

The stark reality of failing stared me in the face. I could see my future slipping away. I needed to rededicate myself—and change my major. I changed to education courses, took nineteen units and pulled a 3.7 average in the spring of 1967 to get my A.A. degree and a grade point average good enough to transfer to a California State school. What surprised me was I did this while having my most successful track season.

During the spring, I received several scholarship offers and visited several campuses. I met with coaches from the University of Southern California, University of California at Los Angles, Southern Methodist University in Texas and San Jose State. Due to the one semester of bad grades, a state college was the best option so I chose San Jose State. My choice was not only because of my grade point average. I knew San Jose State was going to be the best opportunity for success on the track as well as the classroom. Looking back now, the four years of running leading up to that choice were crucial in the process of earning a track scholarship to San Jose State University.

Although my times were not world class, they were credible enough to give me entry into the inner circle of the San Jose State track team. My dream was to run a four-minute mile. Having run 4:09.9 as a college sophomore, I felt I had a chance to drop my time closer to the four-minute mark. However, during that era, a four-minute mile would have been good, but a long way off from the best times being run then. Jim Ryun was running 3:53, with many others in hot pursuit. But a four-minute mile would have been a great personal accomplishment. More importantly, I enjoyed competing. I felt best when I was doing what came natural. But there were a few more surprises ahead of me after transferring to San Jose State.

I soon discovered there is a big difference between running in junior college meets and NCAA Division One meets. The jump from community college competition to the NCAA level of competition was huge with the competition being much more intense.

I will never forget preparing for my first dual meet at San

Jose State. The meet was against Stanford at Stanford in early March of 1968. San Jose State's head track Coach Bud Winter posted a list on the board in the locker room of projected winning times in the upcoming meet. At first I laughed at the predicted mile time and then I felt like I was going to throw-up.

Coach Winter said the time needed to win the mile was going to be 4:06. Ouch! My all-time best was more than three seconds slower than the projected winning time of the very first meet of the season. I first felt disbelief, and then I got queasy in my stomach. In community college, I could start out easy and run in the 4:20's early in the season and then work on lowering my time for the important meets in May and June. Not here.

Coach was right on. The winning time was 4:06.4. I ran 4:12.2 for 5th place and out of the money, but still it was the fastest time I had ever run in early March. The intensity of competition at the NCAA Division One level was a big shock to me. Wow! This was not going to be easy. I had been used to either winning or placing 2nd in most of the races I had run in the past. Winning was not going to be a big part of my running career at San Jose State.

In two years of meets, I won only one race for San Jose State. The one win came in a home dual meet against the University of Washington. In 1969, I beat a runner named Bill Smart running 4:09.2 to his 4:09.5. My last competitive mile race was at the 1969 Pacific Coast Conference finals in Long Beach where I finished 2nd one more time. Ironically, Tim Danielson, now running for San Diego State, got me again.

Appendix 9
What is your Story?

I have discovered that many people, people of all races, have a story of an encounter with racism. I find the stories fascinating. Here are some examples that have come my way in preparing this book and getting feedback from friends.

BOB

Bob, seventy-eight, was raised in a small town in Indiana that was void of any minorities. He had no exposure to what life was like for the black people in the south until he went to college in South Carolina in the early 1950s. He recounts a story of his first awareness of the Jim Crow laws that dominated the Southern states and that he was totally unaware of. Wikipedia tells us that "The Jim Crow laws were state and local laws in the United States enacted between 1876 and 1965. They mandated de jure racial segregation in all public facilities, with a supposedly 'separate but equal' status for black Americans. In reality, this led to treatment and accommodations that were usually inferior to those provided for white Americans, systematizing a number of economic, educational and social disadvantages." (http://en.wikipedia.org/wiki/Jim-Crow-laws)

Bob stated, "When I arrived in the South, I had no car and depended on public transportation to get around. I climbed on a local bus to discover that there was only one other passenger, a black man sitting in the back. I walked to the back and sat near him for no other reason that it just seemed like the thing to do.

"The man, who was much older than me, spoke to me and said, 'You are not from around here are you?' No, I am from a small town in Indiana. 'That is what I thought. Do you see that white line on the floor of the bus about half way back?' Of course I did. He said, 'don't ever cross that line again or you could get into big trouble. You are lucky today that there is no one else on the bus, but no one would be happy with what you did. I appreciate the company, but for your own safety, don't do it again.'

"I followed his advice for the remainder of my time in the south, but was saddened by the situation."

LARRY

Larry, fifty-seven, was raised in Downey, California and had very little contact with any blacks during his youth, except for a few little league baseball games against teams from Watts in South Central Los Angeles. Larry joined the Army in 1971 and was stationed in Columbus, Georgia along with a high school friend from California. One night the two men went out to get some food and drinks. Here is what happened.

"The restaurant was filled with about forty white men, some of whom were soldiers. Two black soldiers were standing at the bar. I noticed that they were being ignored by the bartender. Every attempt they made to get his attention was met with a cold shoulder. After a few moments, a scuffle broke out between the black soldiers and several of the white customers. The police came immediately and broke it up. They began asking what happened, but no one came forward. So I spoke up and told the officer that I would tell him exactly what happened.

"With the group listening, I explained how the two black soldiers had been ignored and treated poorly by the bartender and that they did not instigate the disturbance. When I finished my story, the officer wanted to speak to my friend and me in private. He said that our support of the black soldiers did not sit well with the crowd and he would personally escort us to our car for our own protection. He encouraged us not to linger and to drive directly back to the Army post.

"To our amazement two car loads of the white customers chased us all the way back to the post."

ART

Art, sixty-four, was raised in Charlotte, North Carolina. He lived in a section of town that was near office buildings and many of the white office workers would park in his neighborhood. When he was seven, his mother was walking him to the store to buy some new shoes. Being black, they were not allowed to go in the front door but had to go around back and down stairs into a basement to buy shoes.

As they were walking toward the store, a white man reading a newspaper approached them from the other direction. Here is what happened.

"My mother tried to get us both out of the way of the man. He was reading and not paying attention to where he was walking. We bumped into him. He got really upset and slapped my mother to the ground with the admonition to never touch a white man again. I was really upset, but being seven years old, there was not much I could do."

ERNESTINE

Ernestine, fifty-something, sang for a Christian traveling group called the Spurlows. They would sing in churches and then stay in the homes of church members before moving on to the next performance. She was raised in California and had never traveled to the South before. Here is her memory.

"While we were in Florida, the group leader could not find any home in one particular town that would take me and the one other black member of the choir. It was really frustrating and it was the first time I had ever experienced anything like that. Finally, one family agreed to take us in, but it was not with a lot of enthusiasm."

What is your story? Email me at speedcity68@yahoo.com with your short story of exposure to racism, either something done to you or something you observed being done to someone else.

Intermedia Publishing Group

Publishing That Works For You

Do you need a speaker?

Do you want Jim Adkins to speak to your group or event? Then contact Larry Davis at: **(623) 337-8710** or email: **ldavis@intermediapr.com** or use the contact form at: **www.intermediapr.com**.

Whether you want to purchase bulk copies of *Life Lessons From Speed City* or buy another book for a friend, get it now at: **www.imprbooks.com**.

If you have a book that you would like to publish, contact Terry Whalin, Publisher, at Intermedia Publishing Group, (623) 337-8710 or email: twhalin@intermediapub. com or use the contact form at: www.intermediapub.com.